WORKING PAPERS

to accompany

ACCOUNTING PRINCIPLES

6th Edition

VOLUME II / CHAPTERS 14-27

JERRY J. WEYGANDT Ph.D., C.P.A.
Arthur Andersen Alumni Professor of Accounting
University of Wisconsin - Madison
Madison, Wisconsin

DONALD E. KIESO Ph.D., C.P.A.
KPMG Peat Marwick Emeritus Professor of Accountancy
Northern Illinois University
DeKalb, Illinois

PAUL D. KIMMEL Ph.D., C.P.A.
Associate Professor of Accounting
University of Wisconsin - Milwaukee
Milwaukee, Wisconsin

Prepared By
DICK D. WASSON M.B.A., C.P.A.
Southwestern College
San Diego State University
University of Phoenix

JOHN WILEY & SONS, INC.
New York • Chichester • Weinheim • Brisbane • Singapore • Toronto

COVER PHOTO   © James Bareham/Stone.

To order books or for customer service call 1-800-CALL-WILEY (225-5945).

ISBN 0-471-39179-4

Printed in the United States of America

10 9 8 7 6 5 4 3 2 1

Printed and bound by Courier Kendallville, Inc.

NOTE TO THE STUDENT

These working papers contain solution forms for all Brief Exercises, Exercises, and Problems in Weygandt, et al., *Accounting Principles*, 6th edition, Chapters 14 – 27 and Appendix C. The working papers also contain solution forms for each Financial Reporting Problem, Comparative Analysis Problem, Interpreting Financial Statements, Exploring the Web, Group Decision Case, Communication Activity, and Ethics Case. There are no working paper solution forms for any of the Self-Study Questions or chapter Questions at the end of each chapter.

In general, the working papers follow the organization of the textbook. To maximize the use of space, however, forms for the Exercises occasionally appear out of order.

1		1
2		2
3		3
4		4
5		5
6		6
7		7
8		8
9		9
10		10
11		11
12		12
13		13
14		14
15		15
16		16
17		17
18		18
19		19
20		20
21		21
22		22
23		23
24		24
25		25
26		26
27		27
28		28
29		29
30		30
31		31
32		32
33		33
34		34
35		35
36		36
37		37
38		38
39		39
40		40

1			
2			
3			
4			
5			
6			
7			
8			
9			
10			
11			
12			
13			
14			
15			
16			
17			
18			
19			
20			
21			
22			
23			
24			
25			
26			
27			
28			
29			
30			
31			
32			
33			
34			
35			
36			
37			
38			
39			
40			

(a) General Journal   J12

Date	Account Titles and Explanation	Ref.	Debit	Credit	
1					1
2					2
3					3
4					4
5					5
6					6
7					7
8					8
9					9
10					10
11					11
12					12
13					13
14					14
15					15
16					16
17					17
18					18
19					19
20					20

(b) Paid-in Capital from Treasury Stock

Date	Explanation	Ref.	Debit	Credit	Balance

(b) (Continued)

Treasury Stock

Date	Explanation	Ref.	Balance	Credit	Balance

Retained Earnings

Date	Explanation	Ref.	Debit	Credit	Balance

(c)

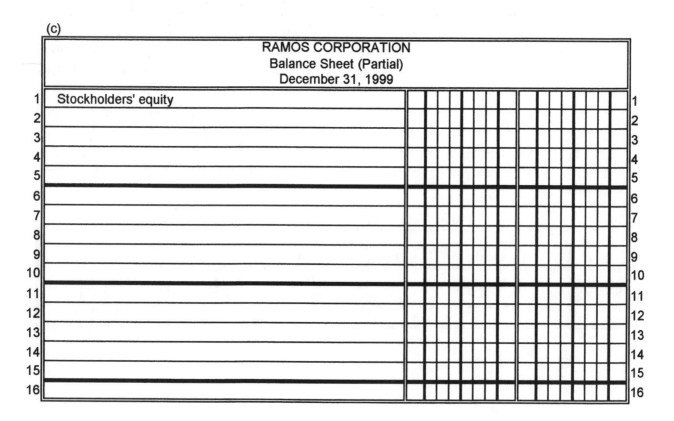

RAMOS CORPORATION
Balance Sheet (Partial)
December 31, 1999

1	Stockholders' equity
2	
3	
4	
5	
6	
7	
8	
9	
10	
11	
12	
13	
14	
15	
16	

(a)   General Journal   J1

	Date	Account Titles and Explanation	Ref.	Debit	Credit	
1						1
2						2
3						3
4						4
5						5
6						6
7						7
8						8
9						9
10						10
11						11
12						12
13						13
14						14
15						15
16						16
17						17
18						18
19						19
20						20

(b)

Preferred Stock

Date	Explanation	Ref.	Debit	Credit	Balance

(b) (Continued)

Common Stock

Date	Explanation	Ref.	Debit	Credit	Balance

Paid-in Capital in Excess of Par Value-Preferred Stock

Date	Explanation	Ref.	Debit	Credit	Balance

Paid-in Capital in Excess of Stated Value-Common Stock

Date	Explanation	Ref.	Debit	Credit	Balanace

Retained Earnings

Date	Explanation	Ref.	Debit	Credit	Balance

Treasury Stock-Common

Date	Explanation	Ref.	Debit	Credit	Balance

Paid-in Capital from Treasury Stock-Common

Date	Explanation	Ref.	Debit	Credit	Balance

Name

Section

Date

(c)

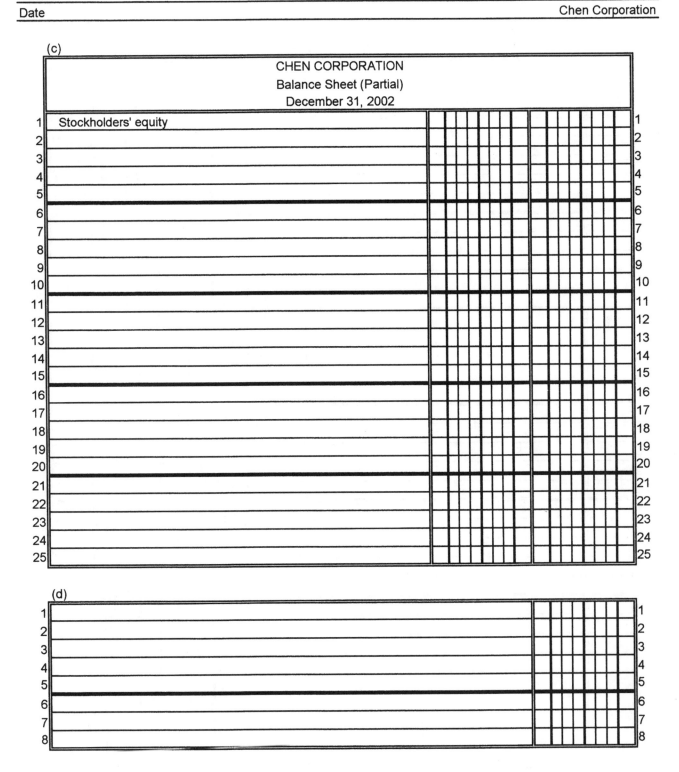

CHEN CORPORATION
Balance Sheet (Partial)
December 31, 2002

Stockholders' equity

(d)

(a) General Journal   J2

	Date	Account Titles and Explanation	Ref.	Debit	Credit	
1						1
2						2
3						3
4						4
5						5
6						6
7						7
8						8
9						9
10						10
11						11
12						12
13						13
14						14
15						15
16						16
17						17
18						18
19						19
20						20
21						21
22						22
23						23
24						24
25						25
26						26
27						27
28						28
29						29
30						30
31						31
32						32
33						33
34						34
35						35
36						36
37						37

(a)

ICELAND CORPORATION				
Balance Sheet (Partial)				
December 31, 2002				
1	Stockholders' equity			1
2				2
3				3
4				4
5				5
6				6
7				7
8				8
9				9
10				10
11				11
12				12
13				13
14				14
15				15
16				16
17				17
18				18
19				19
20				20
21				21
22				22
23				23
24				24
25				25
26				26
27				27
28				28

(b)

1			1
2			2
3			3
4			4
5			5
6			6
7			7
8			8

(a)

1
2
3
4
5

(b)

6
7
8
9
10

(c)

	2000	1999

11
12
13
14
15

(d)

	2000	1999

16
17
18
19
20
21
22

(e)

23
24
25
26
27
28
29
30
31
32

	Lands' End	Abercrombie & Fitch
(a)		
Calculation-		
Book value per share		
(b) Comparison-		
Market value per share		
Book value per share		
(c)		

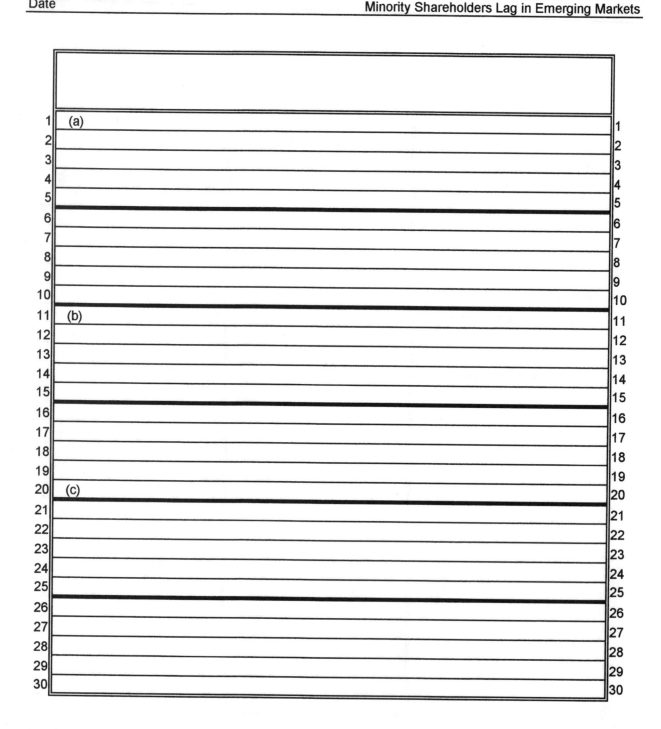

(a)

(b)

(c)

Name

Section

Date

1	(a)	1
2		2
3		3
4	(b)	4
5		5
6		6
7	(c)	7
8		8
9		9
10	(d)	10
11		11
12		12
13		13
14		14
15		15
16		16
17		17
18		18
19		19
20		20
21		21
22		22
23		23
24		24
25		25
26		26
27		27
28		28
29		29
30		30

(a)

(b)

(c)

(d)

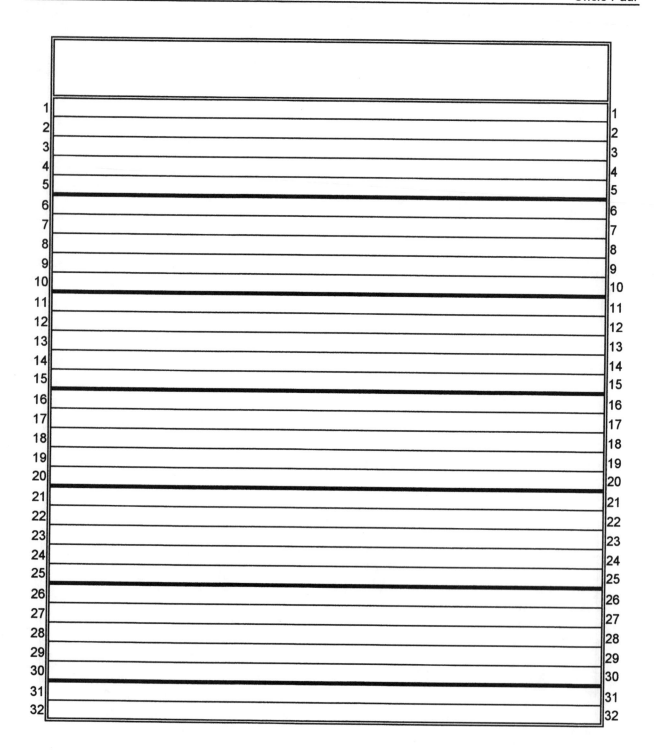

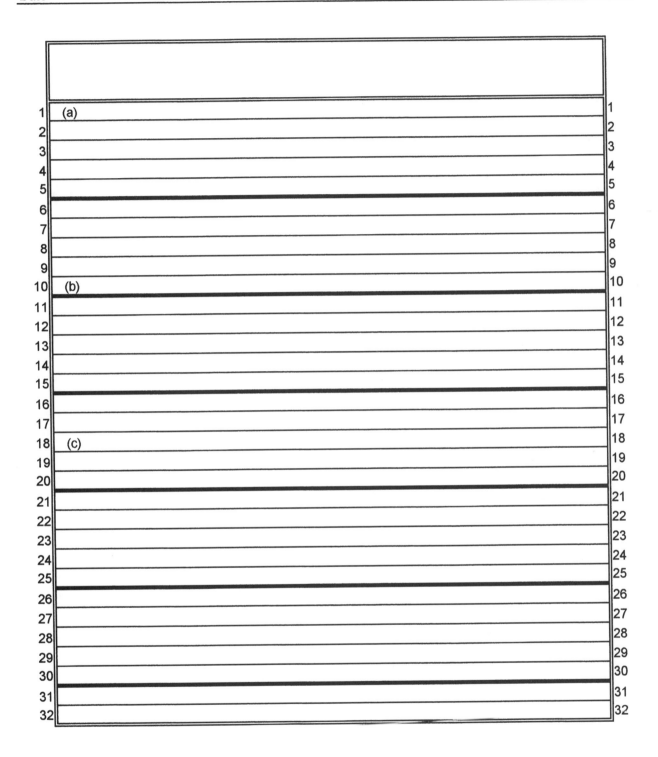

(a)

(b)

(c)

Name

Section

Date

	1
1	1
2	2
3	3
4	4
5	5
6	6
7	7
8	8
9	9
10	10
11	11
12	12
13	13
14	14
15	15
16	16
17	17
18	18
19	19
20	20
21	21
22	22
23	23
24	24
25	25
26	26
27	27
28	28
29	29
30	30
31	31
32	32

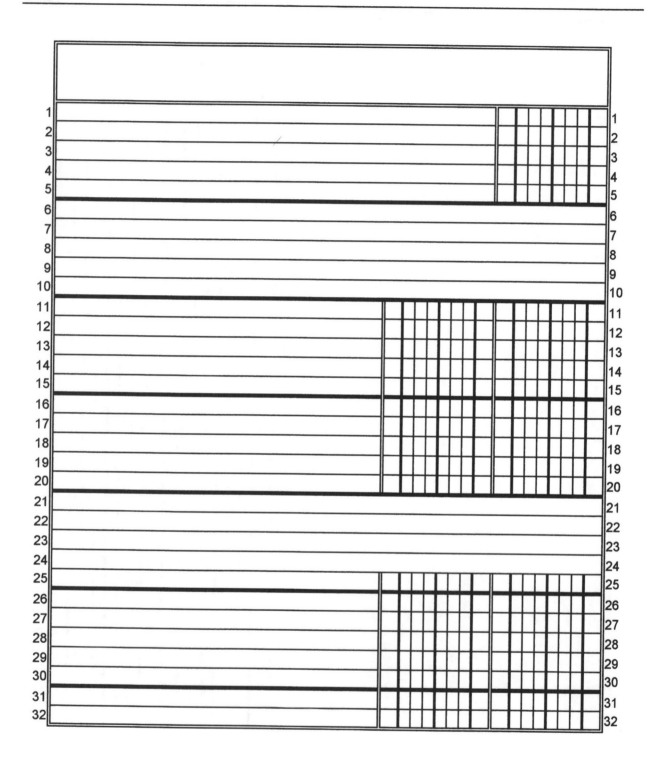

#7

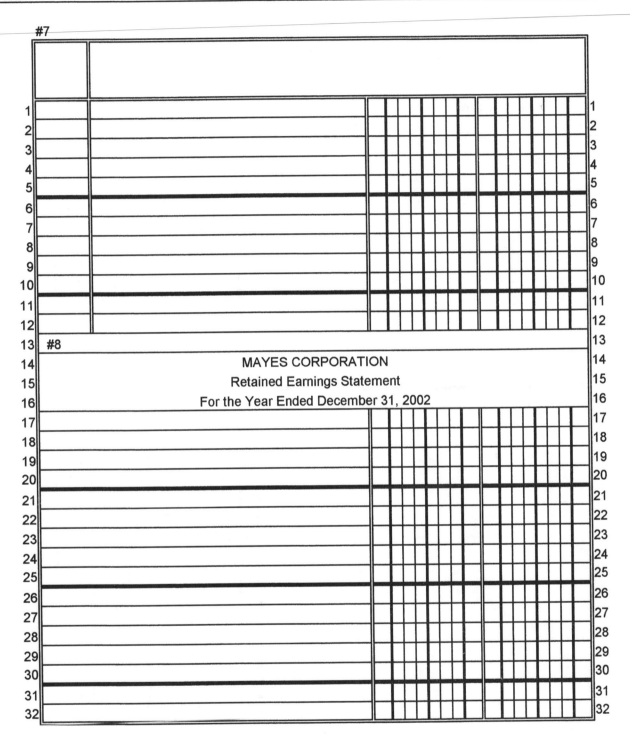

#8

MAYES CORPORATION

Retained Earnings Statement

For the Year Ended December 31, 2002

BYUNG-KEE INC. Balance Sheet (Partial) December 31, 20xx		
Stockholders' equity		

(a)

	RIZZO CORPORATION	
	Income Statement (Partial)	
	For the Year Ended December 31, 2002	
1		
2	Income from continuing operations	
3		
4		
5		
6		
7		
8		
9		
10		
11		
12		
13		
14		
15		
16		
17		
18		
19		
20		

(b)

1	
2	
3	
4	
5	
6	
7	

(a)

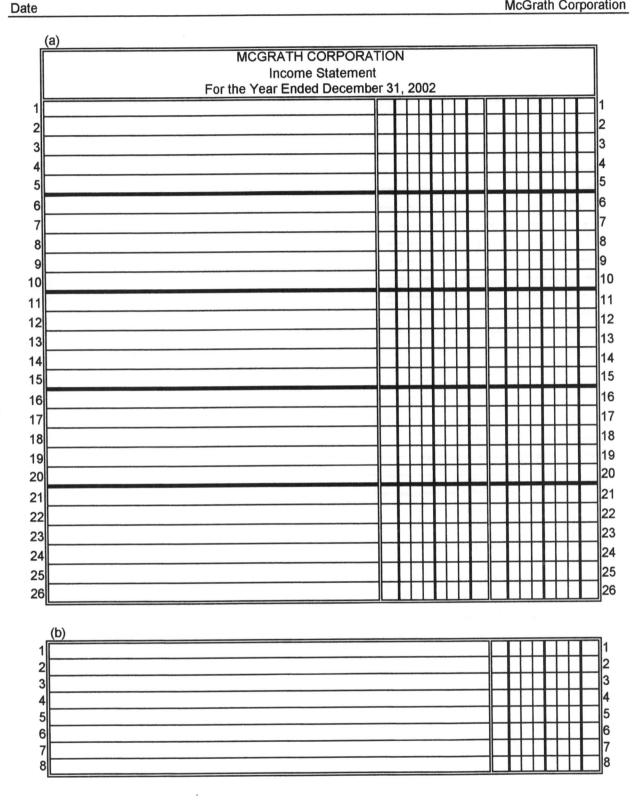

MCGRATH CORPORATION
Income Statement
For the Year Ended December 31, 2002

(b)

(a)

General Journal

	Date	Account Titles and Explanation	Ref.	Debit	Credit	
1						1
2						2
3						3
4						4
5						5
6						6
7						7
8						8
9						9
10						10
11						11
12						12
13						13
14						14
15						15
16						16
17						17
18						18
19						19
20						20
21						21
22						22
23						23
24						24
25						25

(b)

Common Stock

Date	Explanation	Ref.	Debit	Credit	Balance

(b) (Continued)   **Paid-in Capital in Excess of Par Value**

Date	Explanation	Ref.	Debit	Credit	Balance

Retained Earnings

Date	Explanation	Ref.	Debit	Credit	Balance

Common Stock Dividends Distributable

Date	Explanation	Ref.	Debit	Credit	Balance

HARRIS CORPORATION
Balance Sheet (Partial)
December 31, 2002

1	Stockholders' equity	1
2		2
3		3
4		4
5		5
6		6
7		7
8		8
9		9
10		10
11		11

(a)

General Journal

	Date	Account Titles and Explanation	Ref.	Debit	Credit	
1						1
2						2
3						3
4						4
5						5
6						6
7						7
8						8
9						9
10						10
11						11
12						12
13						13
14						14
15						15
16						16
17						17
18						18
19						19
20						20
21						21
22						22
23						23
24						24
25						25

Preferred Stock

Date	Explanation	Ref.	Debit	Credit	Balance

(b) (Continued)

Common Stock

Date	Explanation	Ref.	Debit	Credit	Balance

Paid-in Capital in Excess of Par Value-Preferred Stock

Date	Explanation	Ref.	Debit	Credit	Balance

Paid-in Capital in Excess of Par Value-Common Stock

Date	Explanation	Ref.	Debit	Credit	Balance

Retained Earnings

Date	Explanation	Ref.	Debit	Credit	Balance

Common Stock Dividends Distributable

Date	Explanation	Ref.	Debit	Credit	Balance

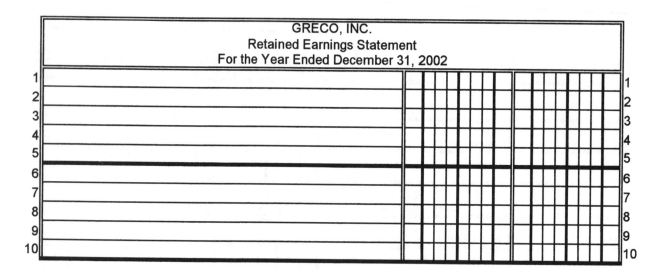

GRECO, INC.
Retained Earnings Statement
For the Year Ended December 31, 2002

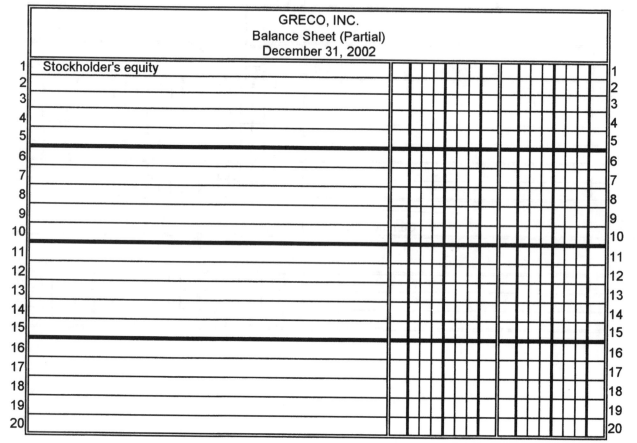

GRECO, INC.
Balance Sheet (Partial)
December 31, 2002

Stockholder's equity

(a)
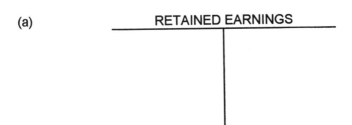
RETAINED EARNINGS

(b)

HEALY CORPORATION
Retained Earnings Statement
For the Year Ended December 31, 2002
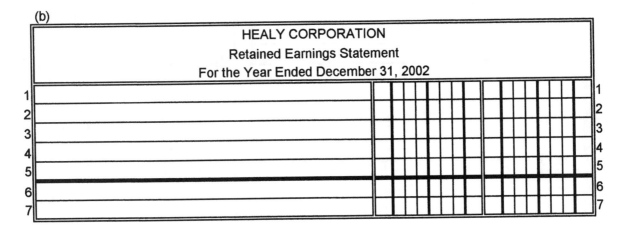

(d) and (e)

(d)

(e)

(c)

HEALY CORPORATION				
Balance Sheet (Partial)				
December 31, 2002				
Stockholders' equity				

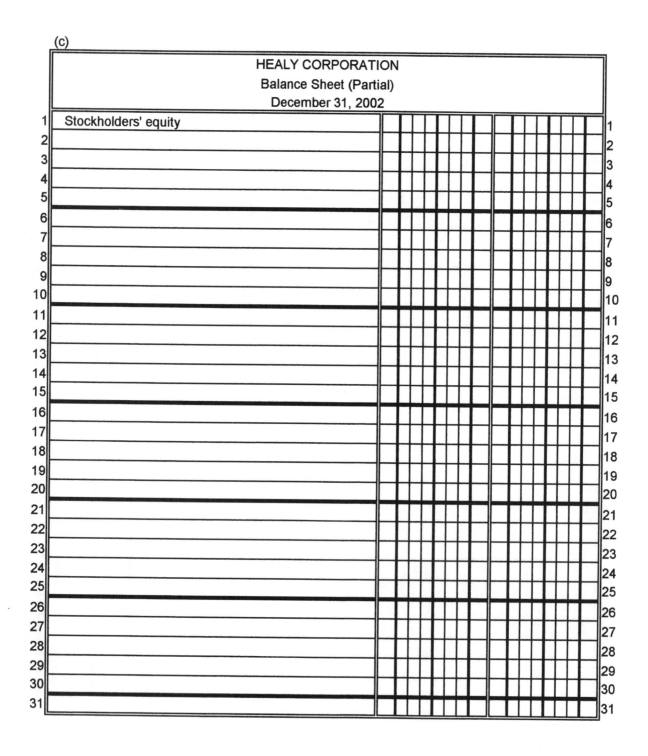

(a)

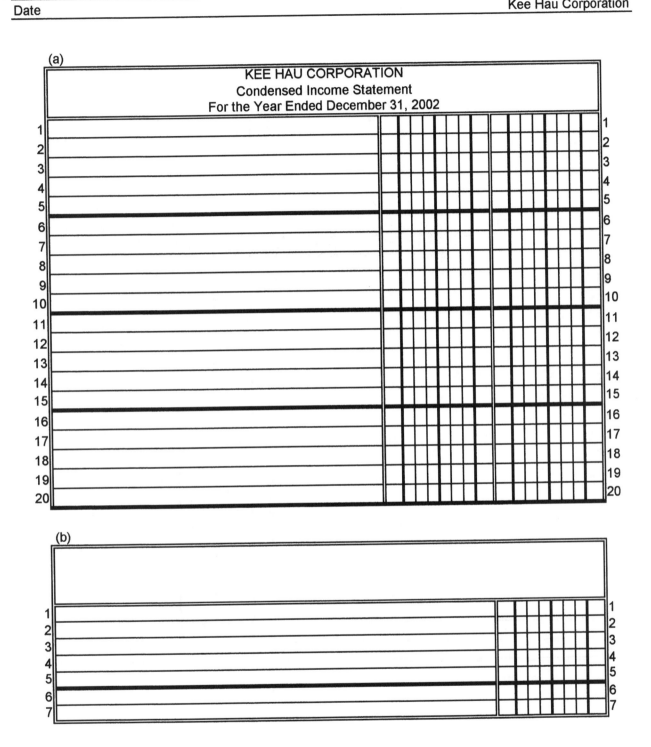

KEE HAU CORPORATION
Condensed Income Statement
For the Year Ended December 31, 2002

(b)

(a)

	HAAK CORPORATION		
	Income Statement		
	For the Year Ended December 31, 1999		
1			
2			
3			
4			
5			
6			
7			
8			
9			
10			
11			
12			
13			
14			
15			
16			
17			
18			
19			
20			
21			
22			
23			
24			
25			
26			
27			
28			

(b)

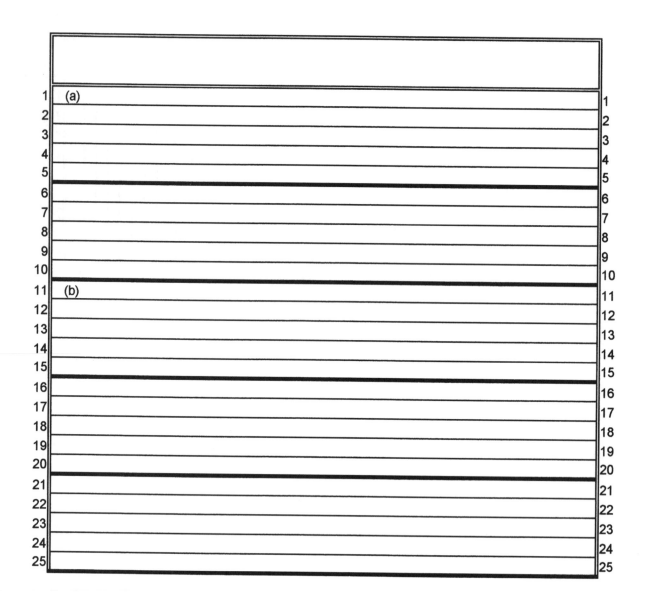

(a)

(b)

(a)

	Lands' End	Abercrombie & Fitch
1		
2 Earnings per share		
3		
4		
5		
6		
7		
8		
9 Return on common		
10 stockholders' equity		
11		
12		
13		
14		
15		
16		
17		
18		
19		
20		
21 (b)		
22		
23		
24 (c)		
25		
26		
27		

(a)

	Current Year	Prior Year
1 Earnings per share		
2		
3		
4		
5		
6		
7		
8		
9		
10		
11		
12		
13		
14		
15		

(b)

16
17
18
19
20
21

22
23
24

(c)

25
26
27
28
29
30
31

(d)

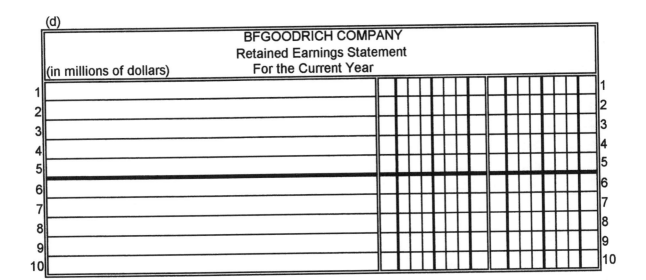

BFGOODRICH COMPANY
Retained Earnings Statement
For the Current Year

(in millions of dollars)

(e)

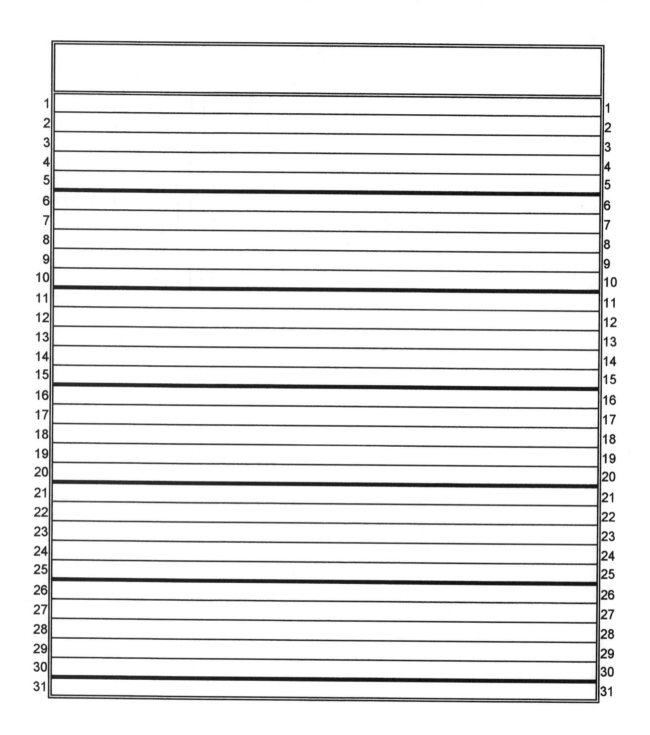

(a)

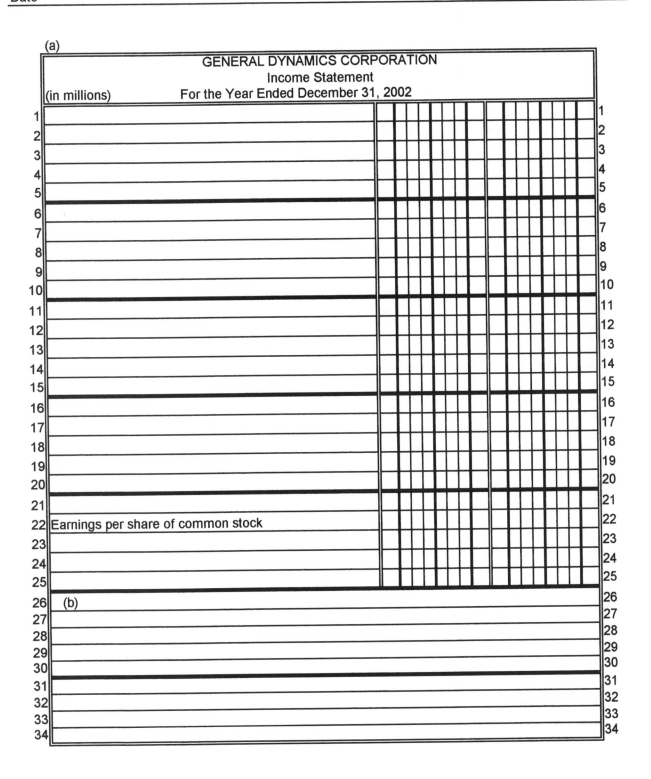

GENERAL DYNAMICS CORPORATION
Income Statement
(in millions) For the Year Ended December 31, 2002

22 Earnings per share of common stock

(b)

1	1
2	2
3	3
4	4
5	5
6	6
7	7
8	8
9	9
10	10
11	11
12	12
13	13
14	14
15	15
16	16
17	17
18	18
19	19
20	20
21	21
22	22
23	23
24	24
25	25
26	26
27	27
28	28
29	29
30	30
31	31
32	32
33	33

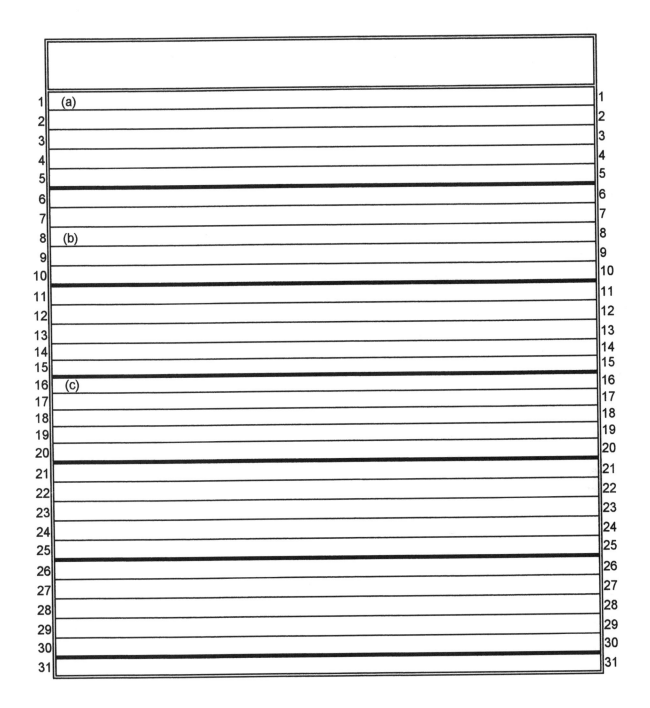

	1			1
1				1
2				2
3				3
4				4
5				5
6				6
7				7
8				8
9				9
10				10
11				11
12				12
13				13
14				14
15				15
16				16
17				17
18				18
19				19
20				20
21				21
22				22
23				23
24				24
25				25
26				26
27				27
28				28
29				29
30				30
31				31
32				32

1						1
2						2
3						3
4						4
5						5
6						6
7						7
8						8
9						9
10						10
11						11
12						12
13						13
14						14
15						15
16						16
17						17
18						18
19						19
20						20
21						21
22						22
23						23
24						24
25						25
26						26
27						27
28						28
29						29
30						30
31						31
32						32

Name

Section

Date

1				
2				
3				
4				
5				
6				
7				
8				
9				
10				
11				
12				
13				
14				
15				
16				
17				
18				
19				
20				
21				
22				
23				
24				
25				
26				
27				
28				
29				
30				
31				
32				

Name

Section

Date

#1	1. Issue Stock	2. Issue Bonds
1 Income before interest and taxes		
2		
3		
4		
5		
6		
7		
8		
9		
10		
11		
12		
13		
14		
15		
16		
17		
18		
19		
20		
21 #2		
22		
23		
24		
25		
26		
27		
28		
29		
30		
31		
32		

#3

1				1
2				2
3				3
4				4
5				5
6				6
7				7
8				8
9				9
10				10
11				11
12				12
13				13
14				14
15				15
16				16
17 #4				17
18				18
19				19
20				20
21				21
22				22
23				23
24				24
25				25
26				26
27				27
28				28
29				29
30				30
31				31
32				32

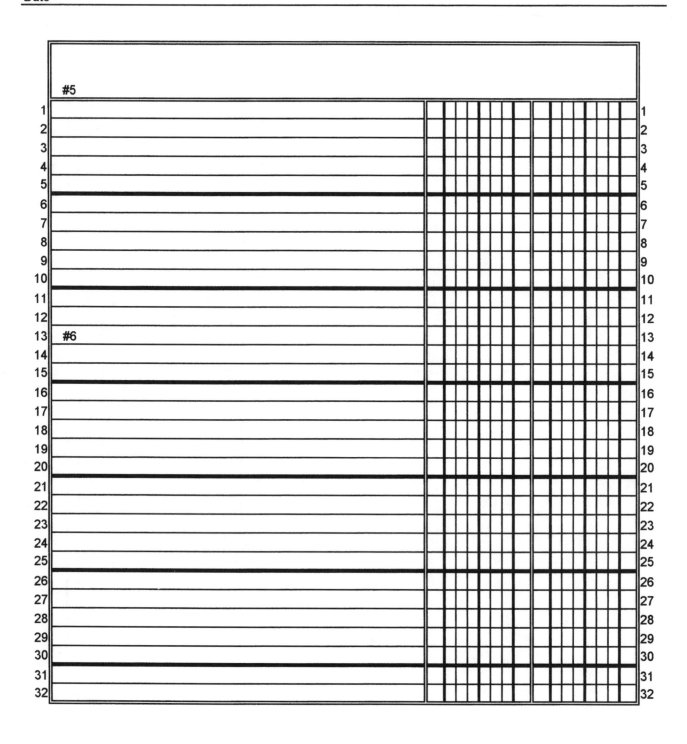

Name

Section

Date

#7

#8

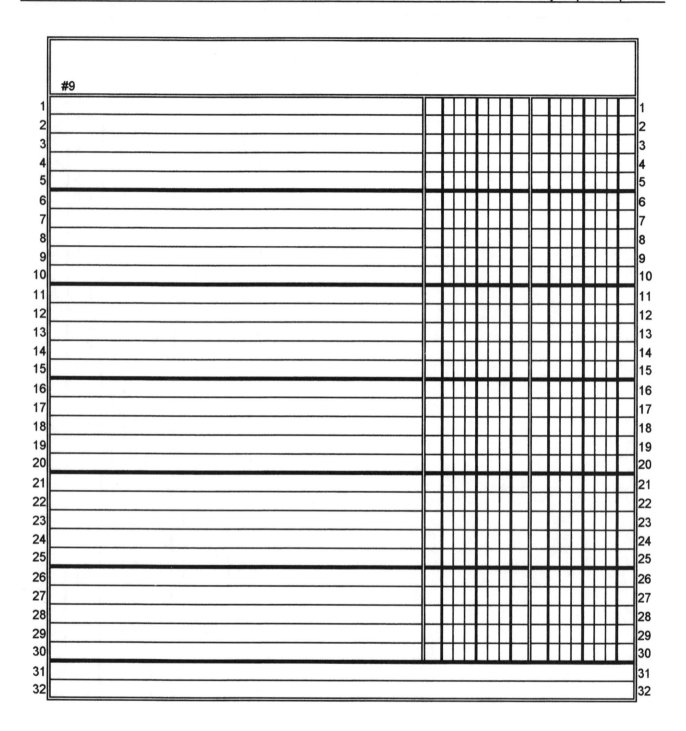

#9

Semiannual Interest Period	(A) Interest to Be Paid (in Cash)	(B) Interest Expense to Be Recorded	(C) Discount Amortization	(D) Unamortized Discount	(E) Carrying Value of the Bonds	
Issue date						1
						2
						3
1						4
						5
2						6
						7
						8
(a) Jan. 1						9
						10
						11
						12
						13
(b) July 1						14
						15
						16
						17
						18
(c) Dec. 31						19
						20
						21
						22
						23
						24

Semiannual Interest Period	(A) Interest to Be Paid (in Cash)	(B) Interest Expense to Be Recorded	(C) Premium Amortization	(D) Unamortized Premium	(E) Carrying Value of the Bonds
1					
2					
3					
4					
5					
6					
7					
8					
(a) Jan. 1 9					
10					
11					
12					
13					
(b) July 1 14					
15					
16					
17					
18					
(c) Dec. 31 19					
20					
21					
22					
23					
24					

General Journal

Date	Account Titles and Explanation	Debit	Credit
(a)	2002		
(b)	2002		

(c)

Premium

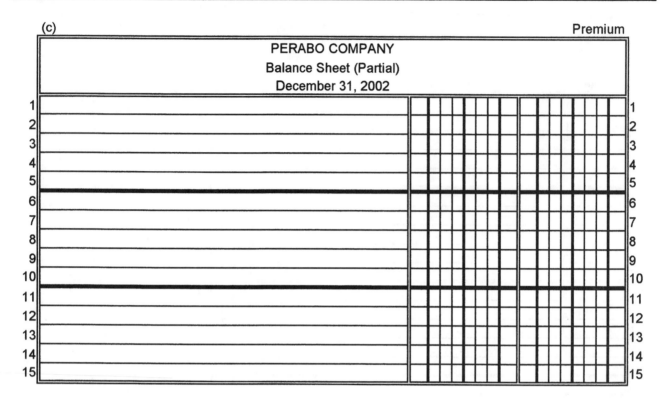

PERABO COMPANY
Balance Sheet (Partial)
December 31, 2002

Discount

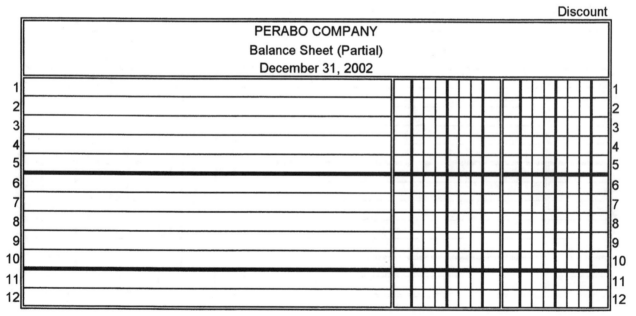

PERABO COMPANY
Balance Sheet (Partial)
December 31, 2002

1	(a)
2	
3	
4	
5	
6	
7	
8	
9	
10	
11	
12	
13	
14	
15	
16	(b)
17	
18	
19	
20	
21	
22	
23	
24	
25	
26	(c)
27	
28	
29	
30	
31	
32	

(a)-(d)

	Date	Account Titles and Explanation	Debit	Credit	
1	(a)	2002			1
2					2
3					3
4					4
5					5
6	(b)				6
7					7
8					8
9					9
10					10
11	(c)	2003			11
12					12
13					13
14					14
15					15
16	(d)				16
17					17
18					18
19					19
20					20
21					21

(e)

EDMONDS CORPORATION
Schedule- Bond Premium Amortization
Effective Interest Method- Semiannual Interest Payments
12% Bonds issued at 10%

	Semiannual Interest Periods	(A) Interest to be Paid	(B) Interest Expense to be Recorded	(C) Premium Amortization	(D) Unamortized Premium	(E) Carrying Value of Bonds	
1	Issue date						1
2	1						2
3	2						3
4	3						4

General Journal

Date	Account Titles and Explanation	Debit	Credit
(a)	2002		
(b)	2003		

(b)

ALGONQUIN COMPANY		
Balance Sheet (Partial)		
December 31, 2003		

(c)

(a) and (c)   General Journal

	Date	Account Titles and Explanation	Debit	Credit	
1	(a)	2002			1
2					2
3					3
4					4
5					5
6	(c)				6
7					7
8					8
9					9
10					10
11					11
12					12
13					13
14					14
15					15
16		2003			16
17					17
18					18
19					19
20					20
21					21
22					22
23					23
24					24
25					25
26					26
27					27
28					28
29					29
30					30
31					31
32					32

(b)

Period	(A) Interest to Be Paid (in Cash)	(B) Interest Expense to Be Recorded	(C) Discount Amortization	(D) Unamortized Discount	(E) Carrying Value of the Bonds
Issue date					
1					
2					
3					
4					

(d)

CLOSET COMPANY
Balance Sheet (Partial)
December 31, 2003

General Journal

	Date	Account Titles and Explanation	Debit	Credit	
1	(a)				1
2					2
3					3
4					4
5					5
6					6
7					7
8					8
9					9
10					10
11					11
12					12
13					13
14					14
15	(b)				15
16					16
17					17
18					18
19					19
20					20
21					21
22					22
23					23
24					24
25					25
26					26
27					27
28					28
29					29
30					30
31					31
32					32

(c)

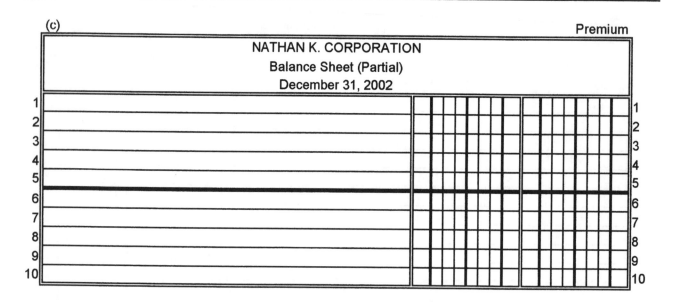

Premium

NATHAN K. CORPORATION

Balance Sheet (Partial)

December 31, 2002

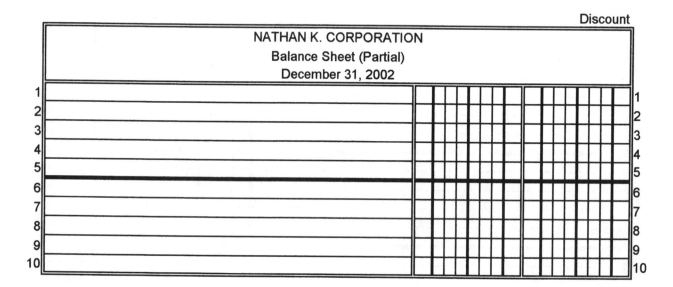

Discount

NATHAN K. CORPORATION

Balance Sheet (Partial)

December 31, 2002

Name

Section

Becky Corporation

Date

General Journal

	Date	Account Titles and Explanation	Ref.	Debit	Credit	
1	(a)					1
2						2
3						3
4						4
5						5
6						6
7	(b)					7
8						8
9						9
10						10
11						11
12						12
13	(c)					13
14						14
15						15
16						16
17						17
18						18
19						19
20						20
21	(d)					21
22						22
23						23
24						24
25						25
26						26
27						27
28						28
29						29
30						30
31						31
32						32

(a)

Semiannual Interest Period	Cash Payment	Interest Expense	Reduction of Principal	Principal Balance
Issue date				
1				
2				
3				
4				

(b)

Date	Account Titles and Explanation	Debit	Credit

(c)

GERE ELECTRONICS

Balance Sheet (Partial)

December 31, 2003

(a)

(b)

(c)

(a)-(d)

	Date	Account Titles and Explanation	Debit	Credit	
1	(a)	2002			1
2					2
3					3
4					4
5					5
6	(b)				6
7					7
8					8
9					9
10					10
11					11
12	(c)	2003			12
13					13
14					14
15					15
16					16
17	(d)				17
18					18
19					19
20					20
21					21

(e)

GODZILLA SATELLITES
Schedule- Bond Discount Amortization
Effective Interest Method- Semiannual Interest Payments
9% Bonds issued at 10%

	Semiannual Interest Periods	(A) Interest to be Paid	(B) Interest Expense	(C) Discount Amortization	(D) Unamortized Discount	(E) Carrying Value of Bonds	
1	Issue date						1
2	1						2
3	2						3
4	3						4

Name

Section

Date   Michelle Pfeiffer Chemical Company

General Journal

	Date	Account Titles and Explanation	Debit	Credit	
1	(a)	2002			1
2					2
3					3
4					4
5					5
6					6
7					7
8					8
9					9
10					10
11		2003			11
12					12
13					13
14					14
15					15
16					16
17					17
18					18
19					19
20					20

(b)

MICHELLE PFEIFFER CHEMICAL COMPANY
Balance Sheet (Partial)
December 31, 2003

1				1
2				2
3				3
4				4
5				5
6				6

(c)

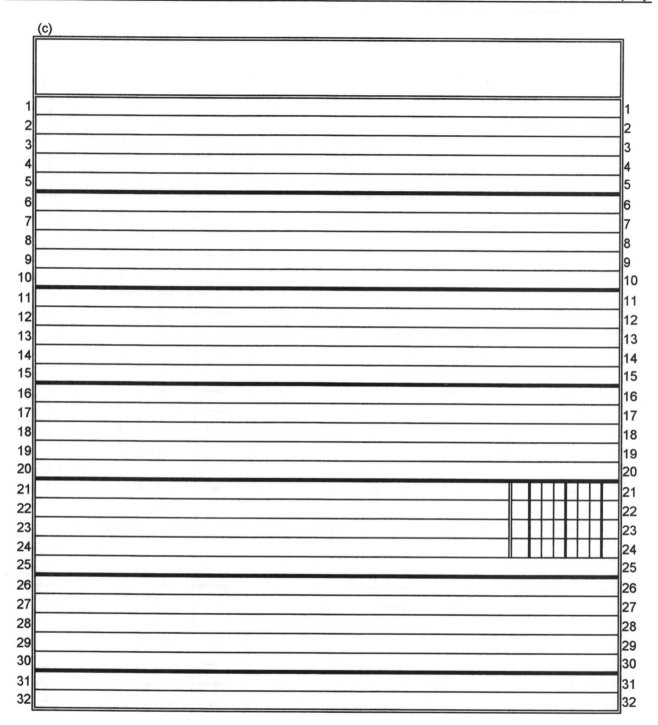

(a)

(b)

(c)

Name

Section

Date

	Lands' End	Abercrombie & Fitch
(a)		
Debt to total assets		
Times interest earned		
(b)		

(c)

	(a)	
1		1
2		2
3		3
4		4
5		5
6		6
7		7
8		8
9		9
10		10
11		11
12	(b)	12
13		13
14		14
15		15
16		16
17		17
18		18
19		19
20		20
21		21
22		22
23		23
24		24
25		25
26		26
27		27
28		28
29		29
30		30
31		31
32		32

1	(a)	1
2		2
3		3
4		4
5	(b)	5
6		6
7		7
8		8
9		9
10		10
11		11
12		12
13		13
14		14
15	(c)	15
16		16
17		17
18		18
19		19
20		20
21		21
22		22
23		23
24		24
25		25
26		26
27		27
28		28
29		29
30		30
31		31
32		32

Name

Section

Date

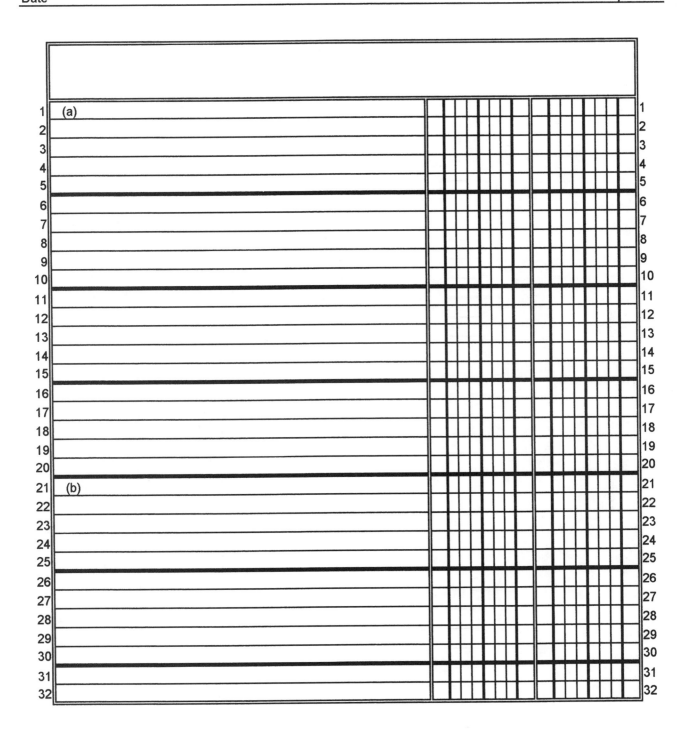

(a)

(b)

(c)

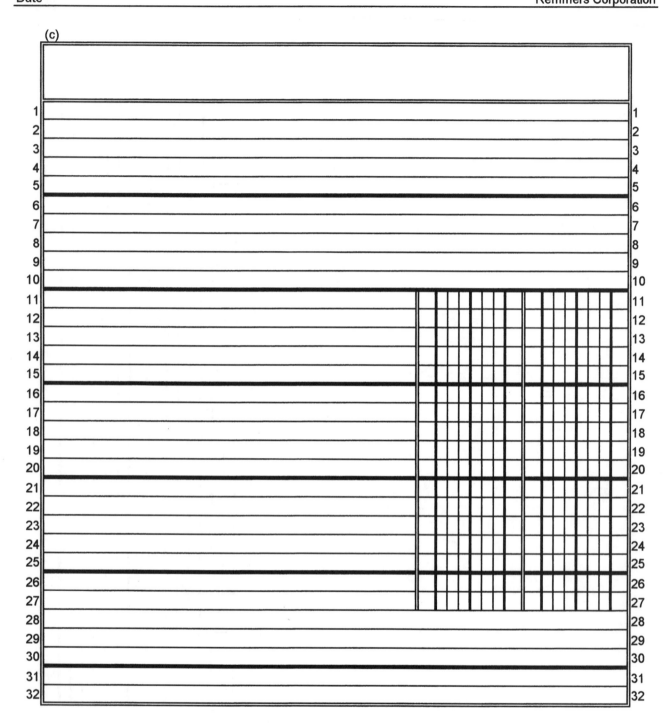

Name

Section

Date

1	1
2	2
3	3
4	4
5	5
6	6
7	7
8	8
9	9
10	10
11	11
12	12
13	13
14	14
15	15
16	16
17	17
18	18
19	19
20	20
21	21
22	22
23	23
24	24
25	25
26	26
27	27
28	28
29	29
30	30
31	31
32	32

(a)

(b)

(c)

Name

Section

Date

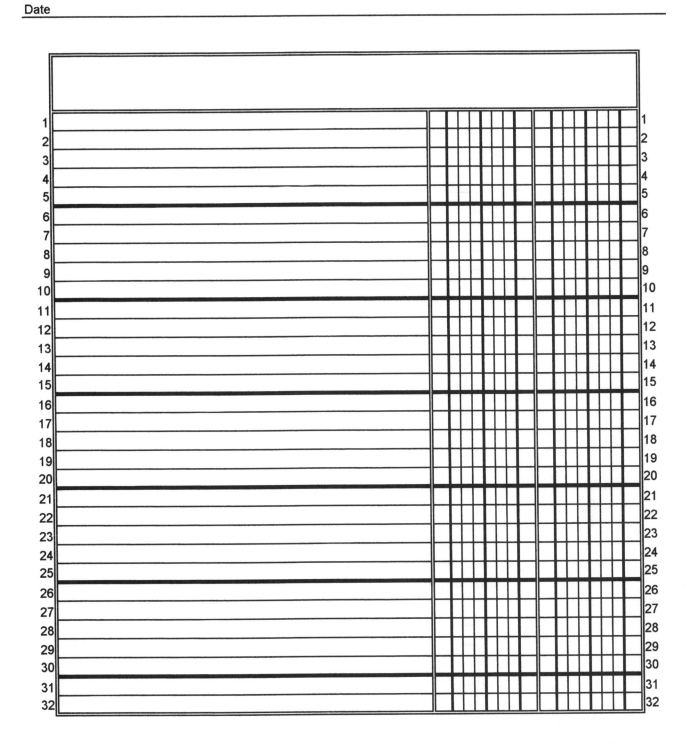

Section

Date

1									1
2									2
3									3
4									4
5									5
6									6
7									7
8									8
9									9
10									10
11									11
12									12
13									13
14									14
15									15
16									16
17									17
18									18
19									19
20									20
21									21
22									22
23									23
24									24
25									25
26									26
27									27
28									28
29									29
30									30
31									31
32									32

	Date	Account Titles and Explanation	Debit	Credit	
1	#1				1
2					2
3					3
4					4
5					5
6					6
7					7
8					8
9					9
10					10
11					11
12					12
13					13
14					14
15					15
16	#2 (a)				16
17					17
18					18
19					19
20					20
21					21
22					22
23					23
24					24
25					25
26					26
27					27
28					28
29					29
30					30
31	(b)				31
32					32

	Date	Account Titles and Explanation	Debit	Credit	
1	#3				1
2					2
3					3
4					4
5					5
6					6
7					7
8					8
9					9
10					10
11					11
12					12
13					13
14					14
15					15
16	#4 (a)				16
17					17
18					18
19					19
20					20
21					21
22					22
23					23
24					24
25					25
26					26
27					27
28	(b)				28
29					29
30					30
31					31
32					32

(a) and (b)

General Journal

	Date	Account Titles and Explanation	Debit	Credit	
1	(a)				1
2					2
3					3
4					4
5					5
6					6
7					7
8					8
9					9
10					10
11					11
12					12
13					13
14					14
15					15
16					16
17					17
18					18
19					19
20					20
21					21
22	(b)				22
23					23
24					24

(c)

MARVEL DAVIS FARMS
Balance Sheet (Partial)
December 31, 2002

1		1
2		2
3		3
4		4
5		5
6		6
7		7
8		8

(a)   General Journal

	Date	Account Titles and Explanation	Debit	Credit	
1					1
2					2
3					3
4					4
5					5
6					6
7					7
8					8
9					9
10					10
11					11
12					12
13					13
14					14
15					15
16					16
17					17
18					18
19					19
20					20
21					21
22					22
23					23
24					24
25					25
26					26

STOCK INVESTMENTS   DEBT INVESTMENTS

Name

Section

Date

(b)

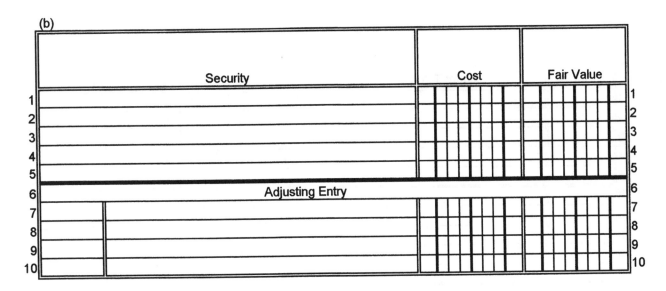

(c) and (d)

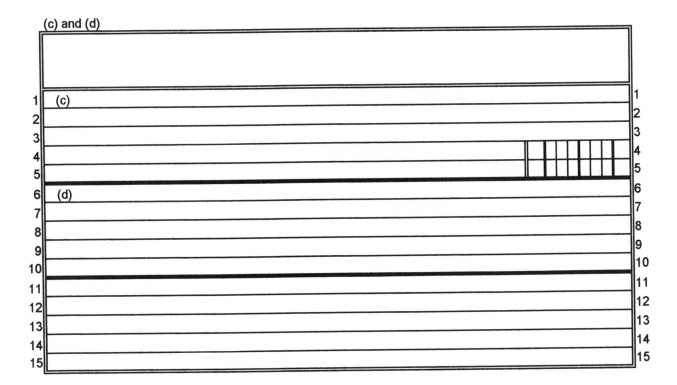

(a)   General Journal

Date	Account Titles and Explanation	Debit	Credit
1			
2			
3			
4			
5			
6			
7			
8			
9			
10			
11			
12			
13			
14			
15			
16			
17			
18			
19			
20			
21			
22			
23			
24			

STOCK INVESTMENTS

(b)

Security	Cost	Fair Value
1		
2		
3		
4		
5		
6		
7		
8 Adjusting Entry		
9		
10		
11		
12		

(c)

MILNER ASSOCIATES
Balance Sheet (Partial)
December 31, 2000

Assets		
Investments		
Liabilities and Stockholders' Equity		
Stockholders' equity		

(a) and (b)   General Journal

	Date	Account Titles and Explanation	Debit	Credit	
1	(a)				1
2					2
3					3
4					4
5					5
6					6
7					7
8					8
9					9
10					10
11					11
12					12
13					13
14					14
15					15
16					16
17					17
18					18
19					19
20					20
21	(b)				21
22					22
23					23
24					24
25					25
26					26
27					27
28					28
29					29
30					30
31					31
32					32

(c)

	Fair Value	Equity Method	
1			1
2			2
3			3
4			4
5			5
6			6
7			7
8			8
9			9
10			10

(a)   General Journal

Date	Account Titles and Explanation	Debit	Credit
1			
2			
3			
4			
5			
6			
7			
8			
9			
10			
11			
12			
13			
14			
15			
16			
17			
18			
19			
20			
21			
22			
23			
24			
25			
26			
27			

(b)   Investment in   Investment in
    McGwire Corporation Common Stock   B. Ruth Corporation Common Stock

(b) (Continued)

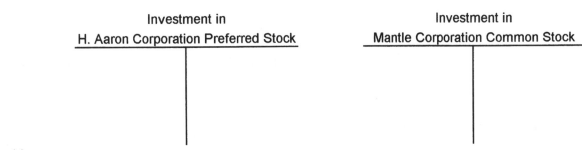

Investment in
H. Aaron Corporation Preferred Stock

Investment in
Mantle Corporation Common Stock

(c)

Security	Cost	Fair Value
1		
2		
3		
4		
5		
6 Adjusting Entry		
7		
8		
9		

(d)

SAMMY SOSA COMPANY
Balance Sheet (Partial)
December 31, 2003

Assets		
1		
2 Investments		
3		
4		
5		
6 Liabilities and Stockholder's Equity		
7 Stockholders' Equity		
8		
9		
10		
11		
12		

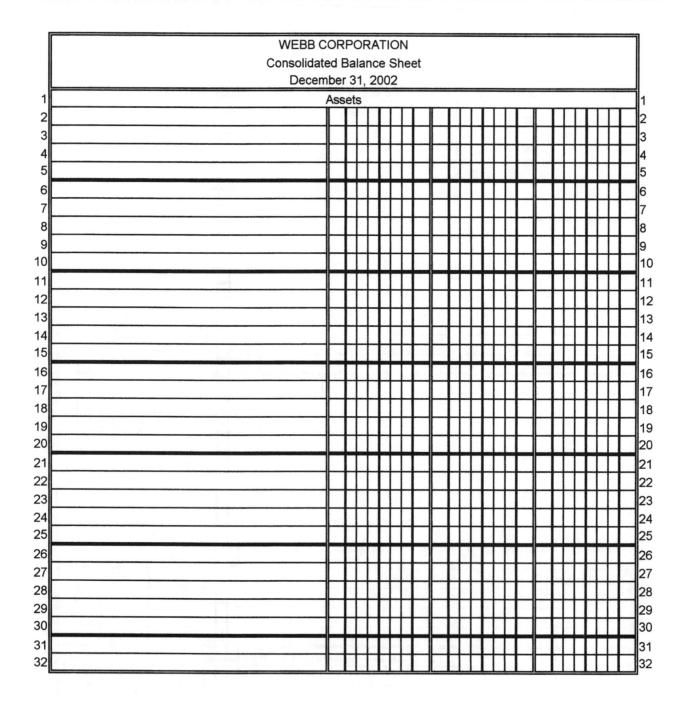

WEBB CORPORATION		
Consolidated Balance Sheet (continued)		
December 31, 2002		
Liabilities and Stockholders' Equity		

Part I

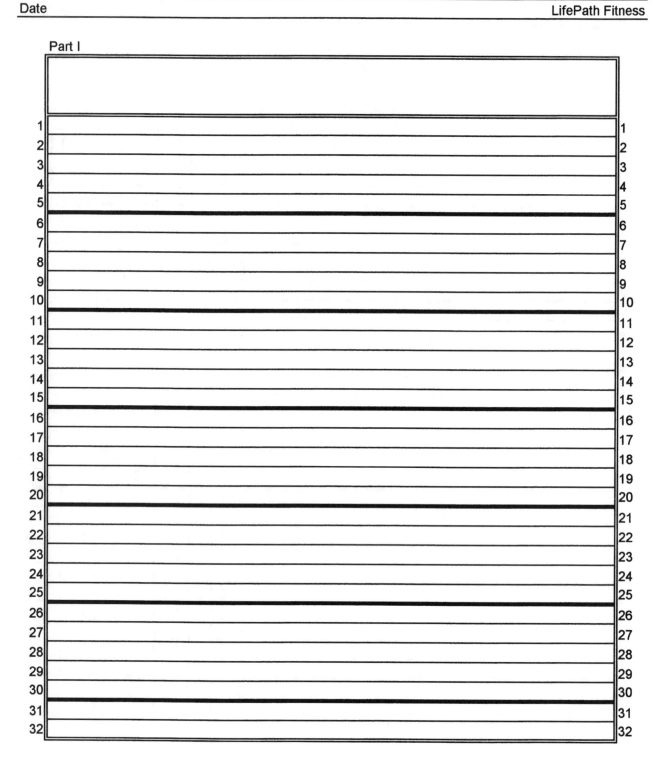

Part I (Continued)

1	1
2	2
3	3
4	4
5	5
6	6
7	7
8	8
9	9
10	10
11	11
12	12
13	13
14	14
15	15
16	16
17	17
18	18
19	19
20	20
21	21
22	22
23	23
24	24
25	25
26	26
27	27
28	28
29	29
30	30
31	31
32	32

Part II

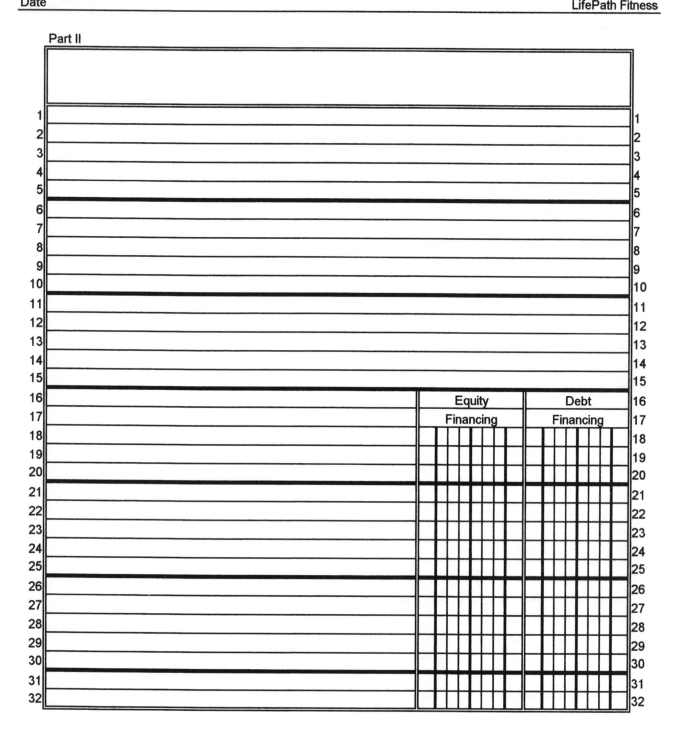

Name

Section

Date

LifePath Fitness

Part III

1		
2		
3		
4		
5		
6		
7		
8		
9		
10		
11		
12		
13		
14		
15		
16		
17		
18		
19		
20		
21		
22		
23		
24		
25		
26		
27		
28		
29		
30		
31		
32		

Part III Continued

	Number of Shares Issued		Total Shares Issued and Outstanding	
1				
2				
3				
4				
5 Part IV				
6				
7				
8				
9				
10				
11				
12				
13				
14				
15				
16				
17				
18				
19				
20				
21				
22				
23				
24				
25				
26				
27				
28				
29				
30				
31				
32				

Part V

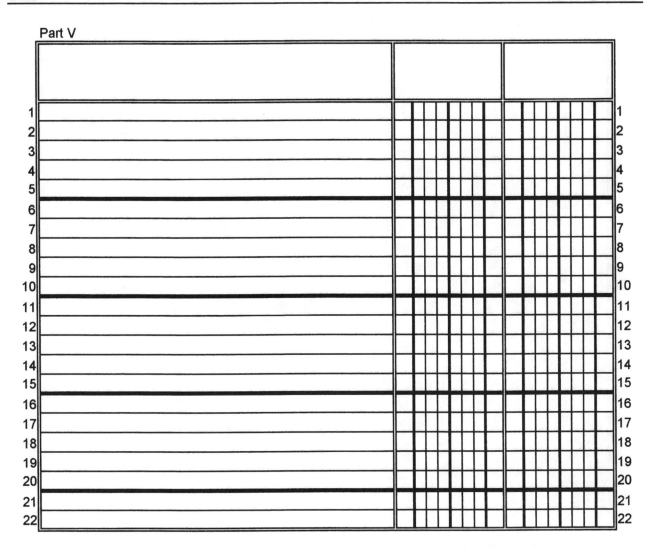

Investment in LifePath

(a)

(b)

	Lands' End	Abercrombie & Fitch
1 (a) Dollars in millions		
2		
3 Cash used for		
4 investing activities		
5		
6 Cash used for capital expenditures		
7		
8		
9		
10		
11 (b)		
12		
13		
14		
15		
16		
17		
18		
19		
20		
21		
22		
23		
24		
25		
26		
27		
28		
29		
30		
31		
32		

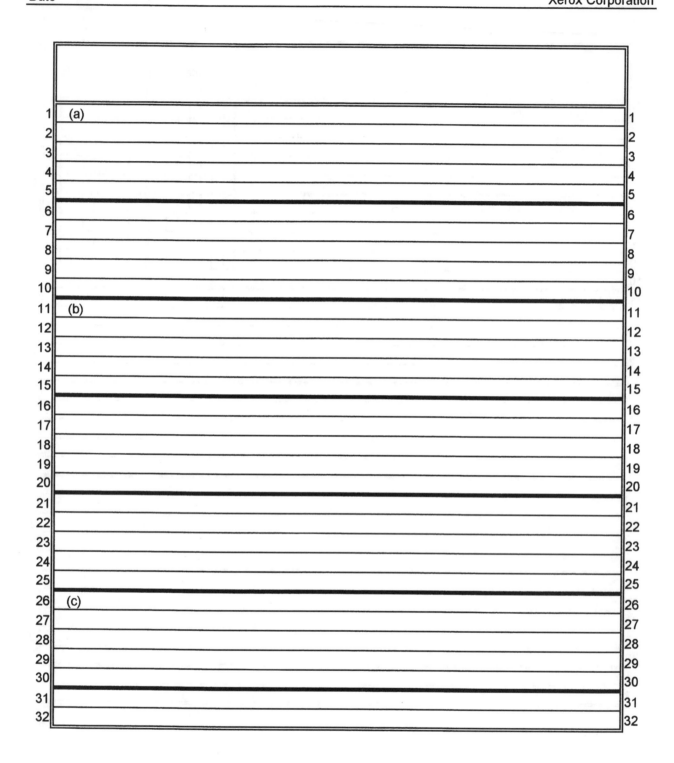

(a)

(b)

(c)

Name

Section

Date

Analysts' Ratings

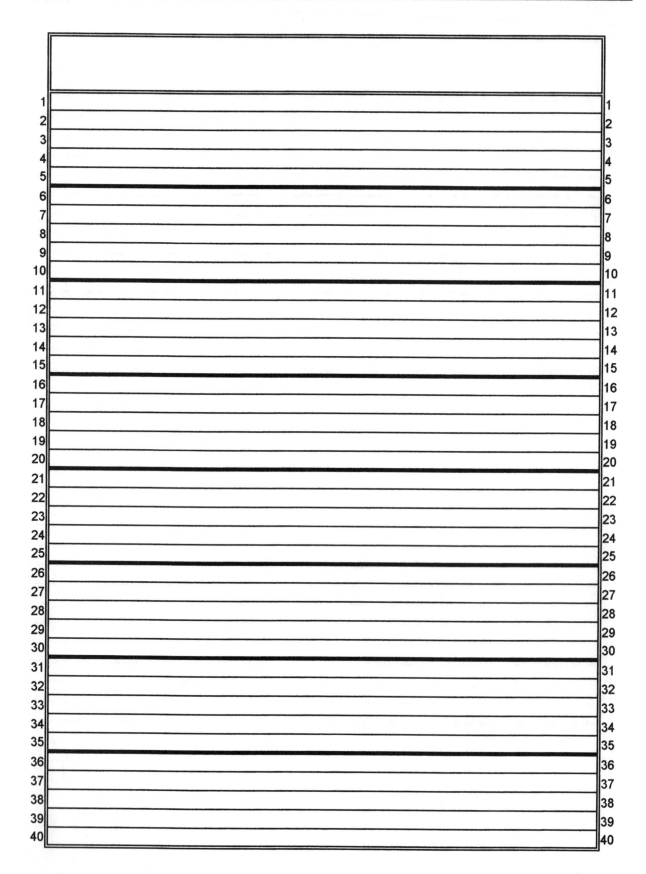

		1
1		1
2		2
3		3
4		4
5		5
6		6
7		7
8		8
9		9
10		10
11		11
12		12
13		13
14		14
15		15
16		16
17		17
18		18
19		19
20		20
21		21
22		22
23		23
24		24
25		25
26		26
27		27
28		28
29		29
30		30
31		31
32		32

	Debit	Credit
1		
2		
3		
4		
5		
6		
7		
8		
9		
10		
11		
12		
13		
14		
15		
16		
17		
18		
19		
20		
21		
22		
23		
24		
25		
26		
27		
28		
29		
30		
31		
32		

Name

Section

Date

	1		1
1			1
2			2
3			3
4			4
5			5
6			6
7			7
8			8
9			9
10			10
11			11
12			12
13			13
14			14
15			15
16			16
17			17
18			18
19			19
20			20
21			21
22			22
23			23
24			24
25			25
26			26
27			27
28			28
29			29
30			30
31			31
32			32

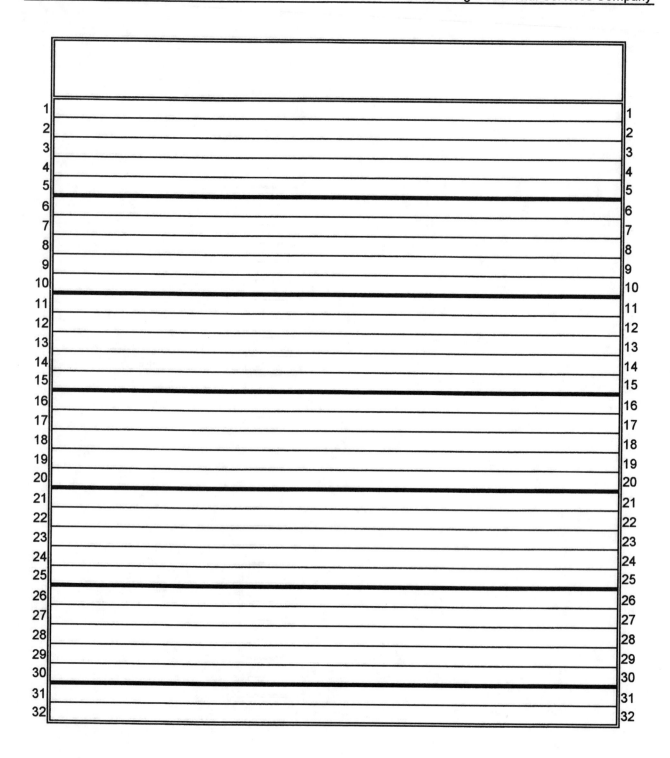

Name

Section

Date

1						1
2						2
3						3
4						4
5						5
6						6
7						7
8						8
9						9
10						10
11						11
12						12
13						13
14						14
15						15
16						16
17						17
18						18
19						19
20						20
21						21
22						22
23						23
24						24
25						25
26						26
27						27
28						28
29						29
30						30
31						31
32						32

Name

Section

Date

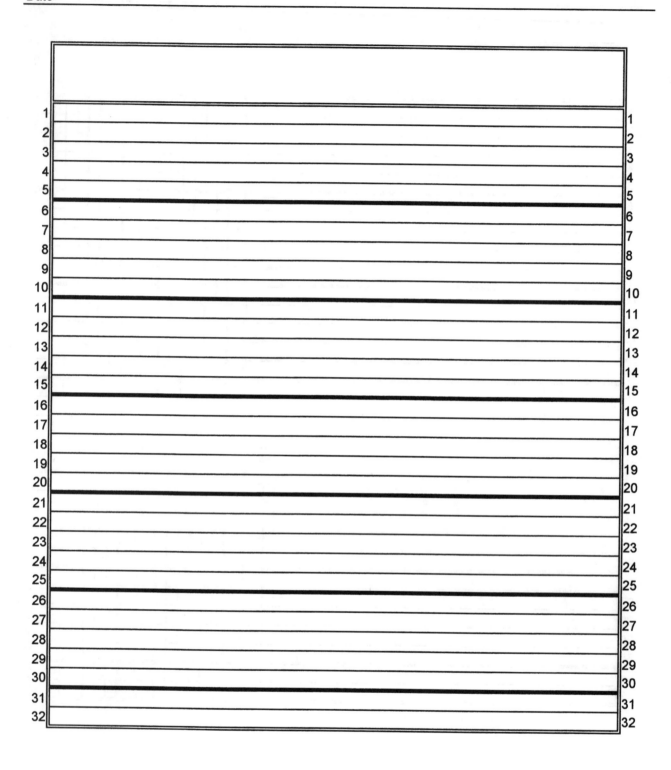

Direct

REBECCA SHERRICK COMPANY
Statement of Cash Flows (Partial)
For the Year Ended December 31, 2002

1	Cash flows from operating activities	
2		
3		
4		
5		
6		
7		
8		
9	Computations-	
10	(1) Cash receipts from customers:	
11		
12		
13		
14		
15	(2) Cash payments to suppliers:	
16		
17		
18		
19		
20		
21		
22	(3) Cash payments for operating expenses:	
23		
24		
25		
26		
27		
28		
29		
30		
31		
32		

Direct

DREAMWORKS INTERNATIONAL CO.		
Statement of Cash Flows (Partial)		
For the Year Ended December 31, 2002		
1 Cash flows from operating activities		
2		
3		
4		
5		
6		
7		
8 Computations-		
9 (1) Cash receipts from customers:		
10		
11		
12		
13		
14		
15 (2) Cash payments for operating expenses:		
16		
17		
18		
19		
20		
21		
22		
23 (3) Cash payments for income taxes:		
24		
25		
26		
27		
28		
29		
30		
31		
32		

(b)

(a)   Direct

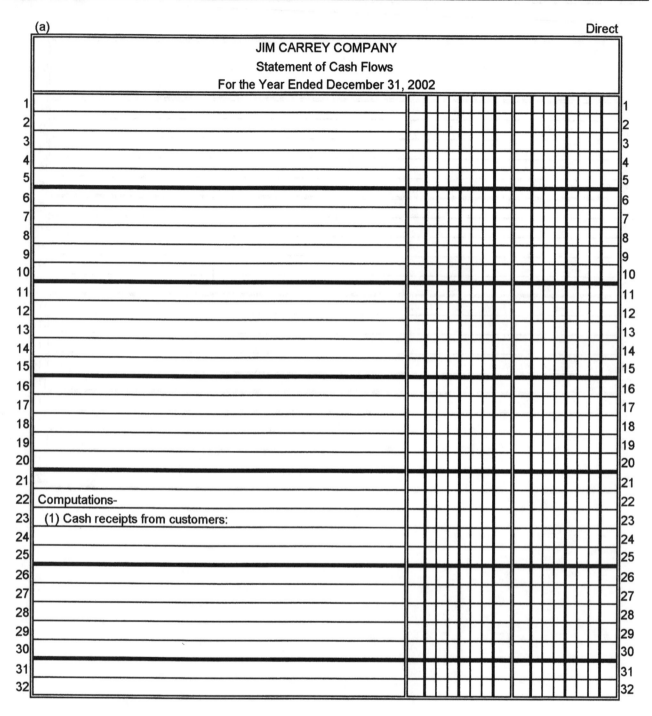

JIM CARREY COMPANY
Statement of Cash Flows
For the Year Ended December 31, 2002

22 | Computations-
23 | (1) Cash receipts from customers:

(a) (Continued)

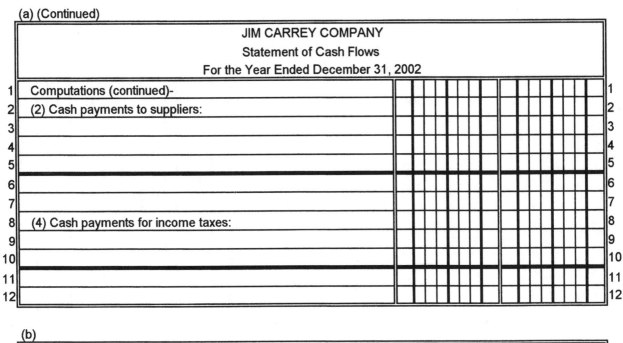

JIM CARREY COMPANY
Statement of Cash Flows
For the Year Ended December 31, 2002

1 Computations (continued)-		
2 (2) Cash payments to suppliers:		
3		
4		
5		
6		
7		
8 (4) Cash payments for income taxes:		
9		
10		
11		
12		

(b)

Indirect

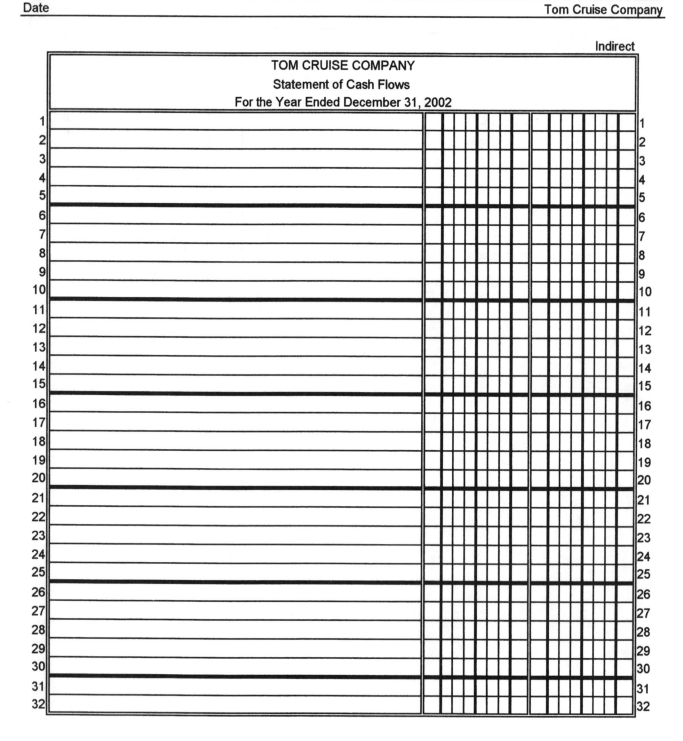

TOM CRUISE COMPANY

Statement of Cash Flows

For the Year Ended December 31, 2002

Direct

	TOM CRUISE COMPANY		
	Statement of Cash Flows		
	For the Year Ended December 31, 2002		
1			
2			
3			
4			
5			
6			
7			
8			
9			
10			
11			
12			
13			
14			
15			
16			
17			
18			
19			
20			
21			
22			
23			
24			
25			
26			
27			
28			
29			
30			
31			
32			

Computations-			
(1) Cash receipts from customers:			
(2) Cash payments to suppliers:			
(3) Cash payments for operating expenses:			
(4) Cash payments for interest:			

Indirect

NICOLAS CAGE COMPANY Statement of Cash Flows For the Year Ended December 31, 2002		

(b)

TOM CRUISE COMPANY
Work Sheet- Statement of Cash Flows
For the Year Ended December 31, 2002

	Balance Sheet Accounts	Balance 12/31/01	Reconciling Items		Balance 12/31/02	
			Debit	Credit		
1	Debits					1
2						2
3						3
4						4
5						5
6						6
7						7
8						8
9	Credits					9
10						10
11						11
12						12
13						13
14						14
15						15
16						16
17						17
18	Statement of Cash Flows Effect					18
19						19
20						20
21						21
22						22
23						23
24						24
25						25
26						26
27						27
28						28
29						29
30						30
31						31
32						32
33						33
34						34
35						35
36						36
37						37

Indirect

BARBARA STRISAND COMPANY				
Statement of Cash Flows (Partial)				
For the Year Ended November 30, 2002				
Cash flows from operating activities				

Direct

BARBARA STREISAND COMPANY			
Statement of Cash Flows (Partial)			
For the Year Ended November 30, 2002			

1	Cash flows from operating activities	
2		
3		
4		
5		
6		
7		
8		
9	Computations-	
10	(1) Cash receipts from customers:	
11		
12		
13		
14		
15	(2) Cash payments to suppliers:	
16		
17		
18		
19		
20		
21		
22	(3) Cash payments for operating expenses:	
23		
24		
25		
26		
27		
28		
29		
30		
31		
32		

Direct

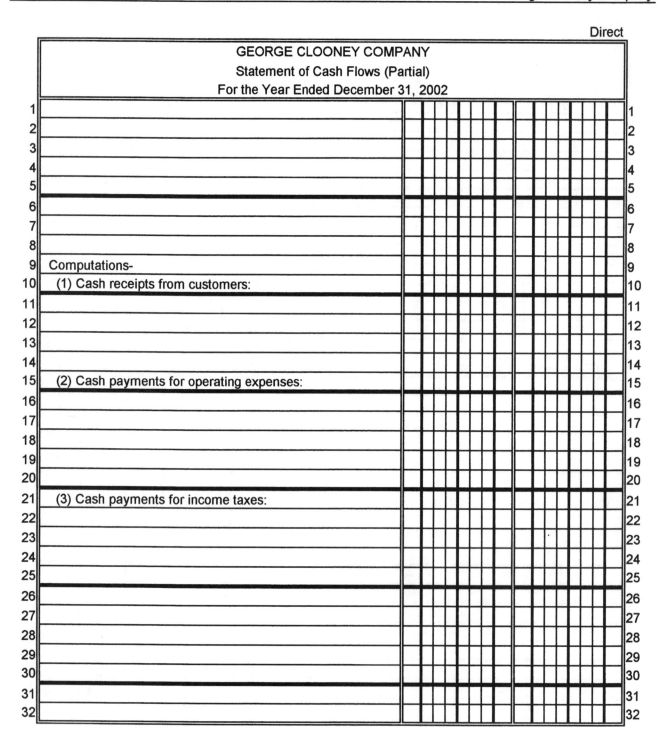

GEORGE CLOONEY COMPANY

Statement of Cash Flows (Partial)

For the Year Ended December 31, 2002

1			
2			
3			
4			
5			
6			
7			
8			
9 Computations-			
10 (1) Cash receipts from customers:			
11			
12			
13			
14			
15 (2) Cash payments for operating expenses:			
16			
17			
18			
19			
20			
21 (3) Cash payments for income taxes:			
22			
23			
24			
25			
26			
27			
28			
29			
30			
31			
32			

Indirect

	GEORGE CLOONEY COMPANY			
	Statement of Cash Flows (Partial)			
	For the Year Ended December 31, 2002			
1	Cash flows from operating activities			1
2				2
3				3
4				4
5				5
6				6
7				7
8				8
9				9
10				10
11				11
12				12
13				13
14				14
15				15
16				16
17				17
18				18
19				19
20				20
21				21
22				22
23				23
24				24
25				25
26				26
27				27
28				28
29				29
30				30

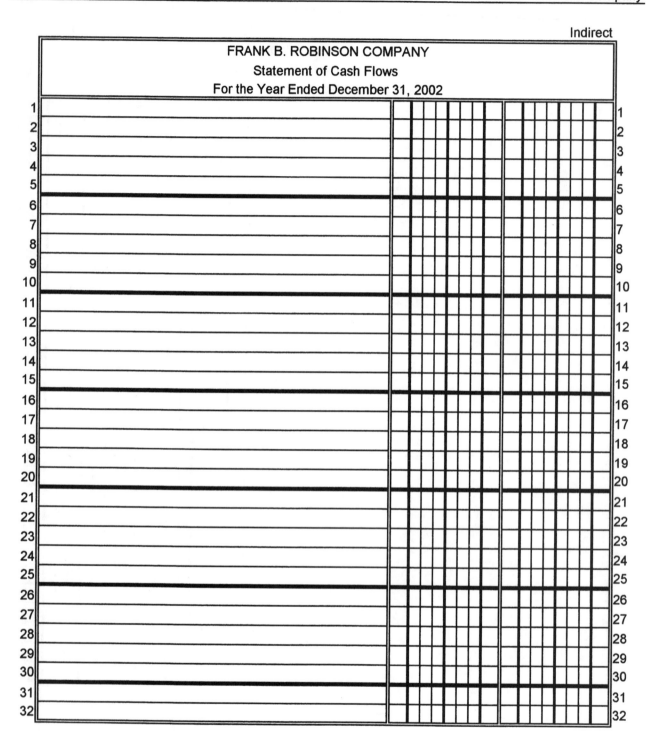

Indirect

FRANK B. ROBINSON COMPANY
Statement of Cash Flows
For the Year Ended December 31, 2002

(b)

Direct

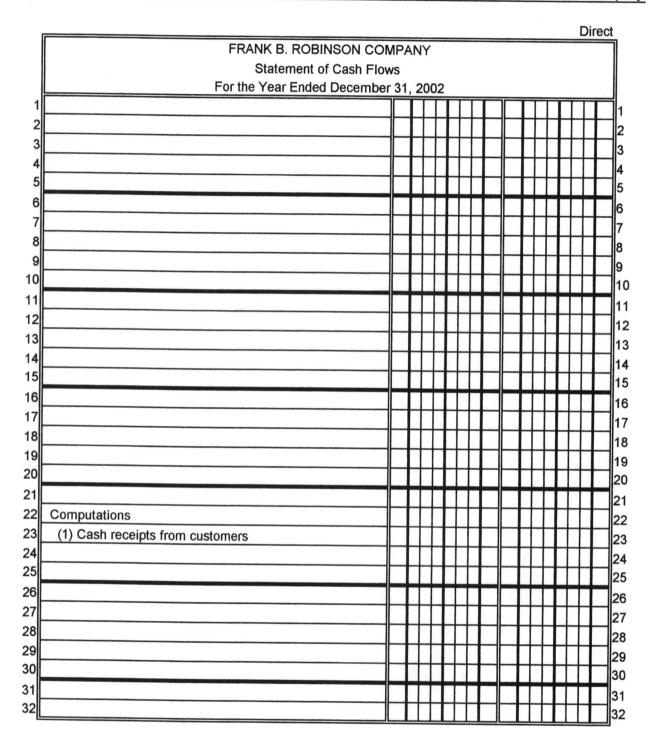

FRANK B. ROBINSON COMPANY
Statement of Cash Flows
For the Year Ended December 31, 2002

Computations

(1) Cash receipts from customers

(a) (Continued)

1	Computations (continued)-		
2	(2) Cash payments to suppliers:		
3			
4			
5			
6			
7			
8			
9	(3) Cash payments for operating expenses:		
10			
11			
12			
13			
14	(4) Cash payments for income taxes:		
15			
16			
17			

(b)

1	
2	
3	
4	
5	
6	
7	
8	
9	
10	
11	
12	
13	

Indirect

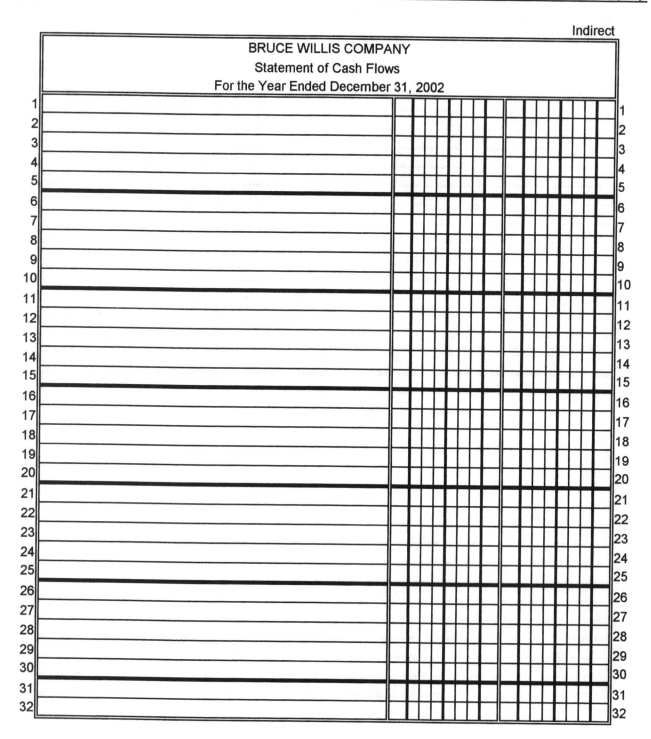

BRUCE WILLIS COMPANY
Statement of Cash Flows
For the Year Ended December 31, 2002

Direct

	BRUCE WILLIS COMPANY					
	Statement of Cash Flows					
	For the Year Ended December 31, 2002					
1						1
2						2
3						3
4						4
5						5
6						6
7						7
8						8
9						9
10						10
11						11
12						12
13						13
14						14
15						15
16						16
17						17
18						18
19						19
20						20
21						21
22						22
23						23
24						24
25						25
26						26
27						27
28						28
29						29
30						30
31						31
32						32

1	Computations-		1
2	(1) Cash receipts from customers:		2
3			3
4			4
5			5
6			6
7	(2) Cash payments to suppliers:		7
8			8
9			9
10			10
11			11
12			12
13	(3) Cash payments for operating expenses:		13
14			14
15			15
16			16
17			17
18	(4) Cash payments for income taxes		18
19			19
20			20
21			21
22			22
23			23
24			24
25			25
26			26
27			27
28			28
29			29
30			30
31			31
32			32

Indirect

DENNIS WEIGLE COMPANY						
Statement of Cash Flows						
For the Year Ended December 31, 2002						

(b)

BRUCE WILLIS COMPANY
Work Sheet- Statement of Cash Flows
For the Year Ended December 31, 2002

Balance Sheet Accounts	Balance 12/31/01	Reconciling Items		Balance 12/31/02
		Debit	Credit	
Debits				
Credits				
Statement of Cash Flow Effects				

	2000	1999
(a)		
(b)		
(c)		
(d)		
(e)		
(f)		

	Lands' End	Ambercrombie & Fitch
(a) Current cash debt coverage ratio:		
Cash return on sales ratio		
Cash debt coverage ratio		
(b)		

(a)

(b)

(a)

(b)

(c)

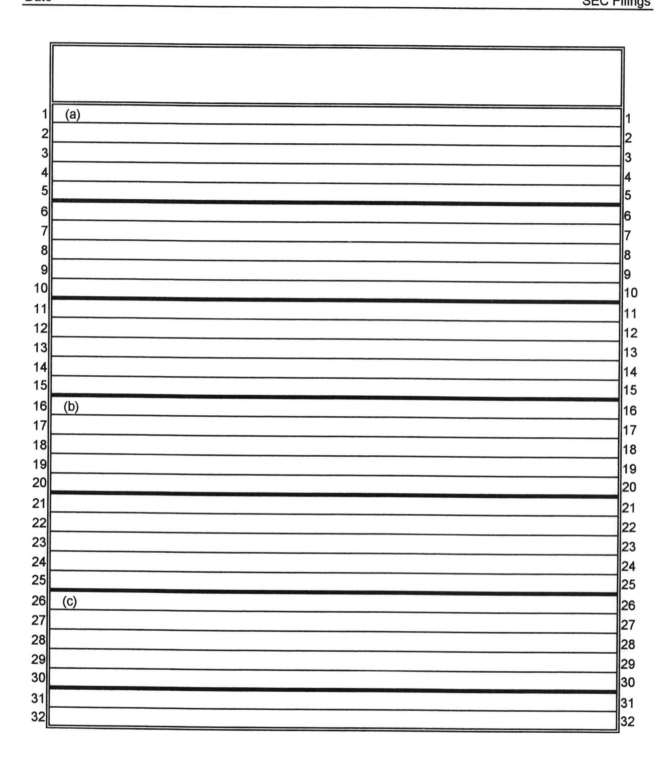

(a)

(b)

(c)

(a)

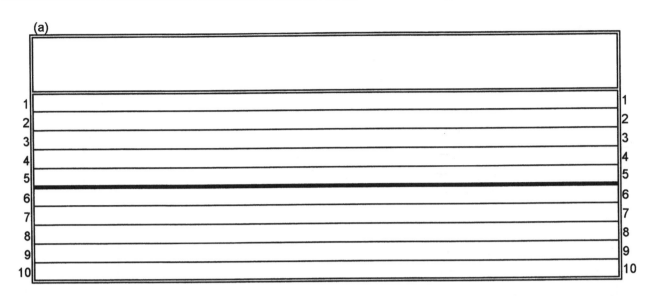

(b)

K.K. BEAN TRADING COMPANY

Statement of Cash Flows

For the Year Ended January 31, 2001

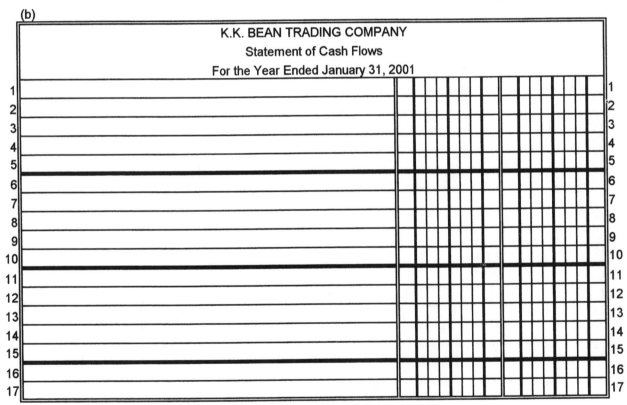

(b) (Continued)

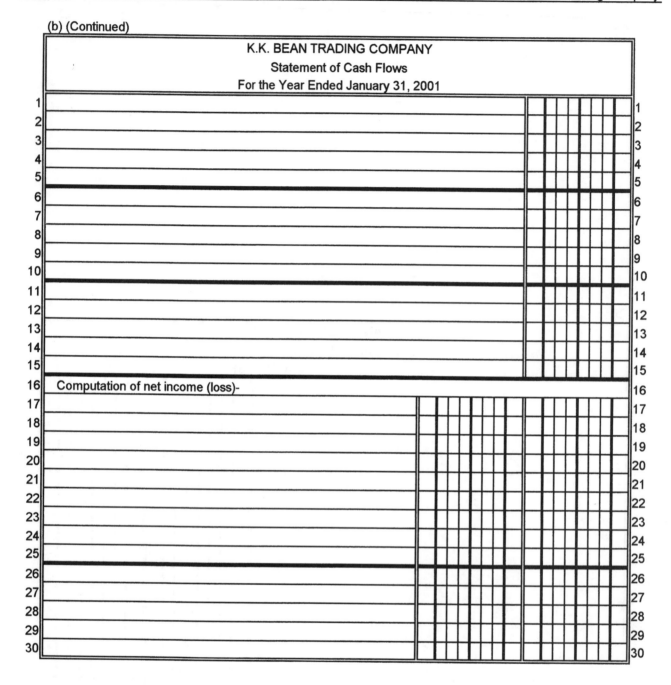

K.K. BEAN TRADING COMPANY
Statement of Cash Flows
For the Year Ended January 31, 2001

Computation of net income (loss)-

Name

Section

Date

1	1
2	2
3	3
4	4
5	5
6	6
7	7
8	8
9	9
10	10
11	11
12	12
13	13
14	14
15	15
16	16
17	17
18	18
19	19
20	20
21	21
22	22
23	23
24	24
25	25
26	26
27	27
28	28
29	29
30	30
31	31
32	32

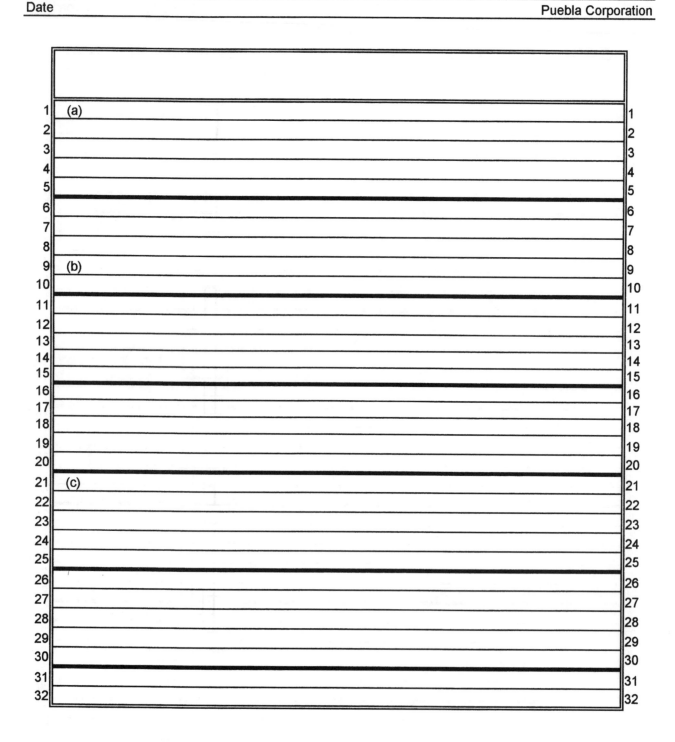

Name

Section

Date

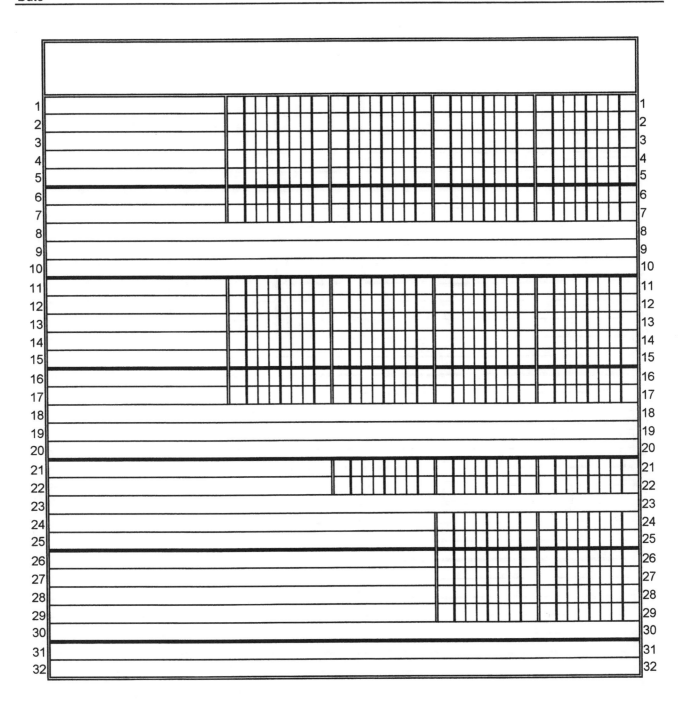

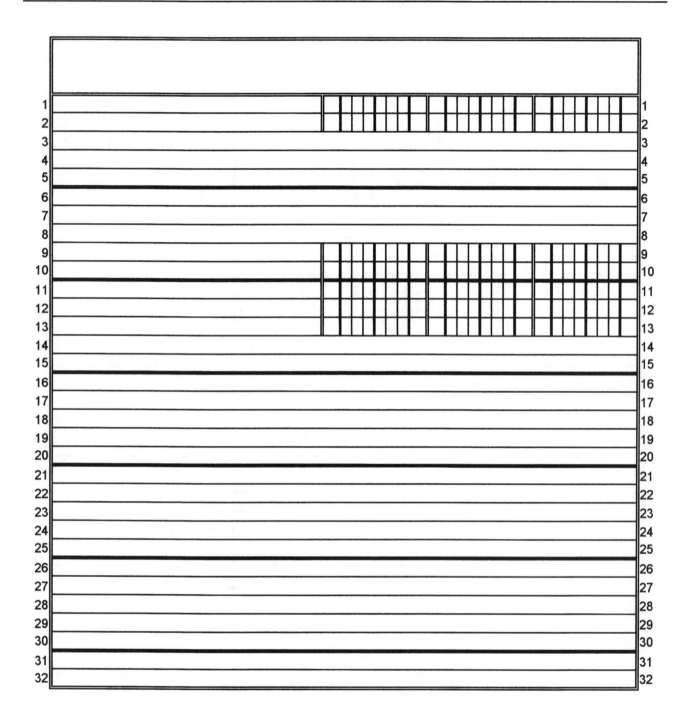

1	1
2	2
3	3
4	4
5	5
6	6
7	7
8	8
9	9
10	10
11	11
12	12
13	13
14	14
15	15
16	16
17	17
18	18
19	19
20	20
21	21
22	22
23	23
24	24
25	25
26	26
27	27
28	28
29	29
30	30
31	31
32	32

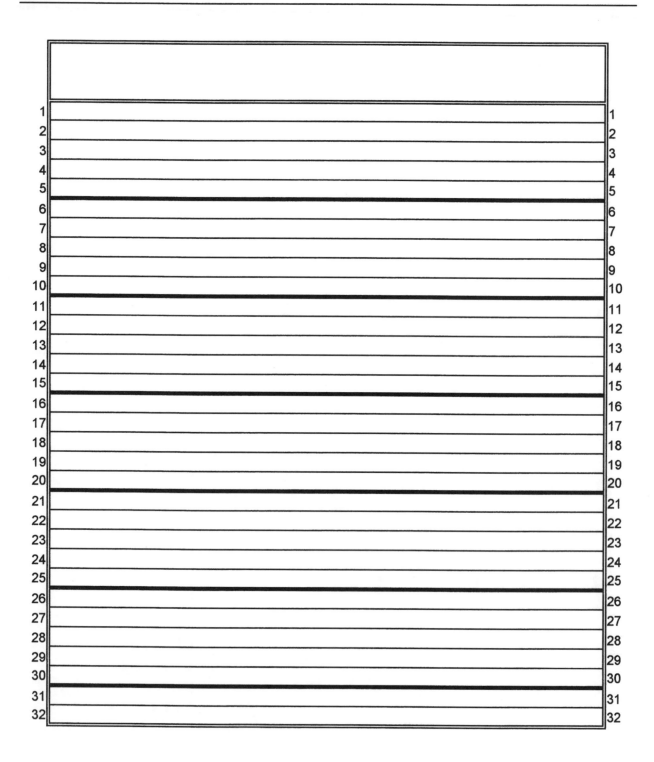

Name

Section

Date

1	#7
2	
3	
4	
5	
6	
7	
8	
9	
10	
11	
12	
13	
14	
15	
16	
17	
18	
19	#8
20	
21	
22	
23	
24	
25	
26	
27	
28	
29	
30	
31	
32	
33	
34	

1	#9	1
2		2
3		3
4		4
5		5
6		6
7		7
8		8
9		9
10		10
11		11
12		12
13		13
14		14
15	#10	15
16		16
17		17
18		18
19		19
20		20
21		21
22		22
23		23
24		24
25		25
26		26
27		27
28		28
29		29
30		30
31		31
32		32
33		33
34		34
35		35

(a)

	MEXICALLI COMPANY Ratio Analysis		
	2002	2003	Change
1 LIQUIDITY			
2 Current Ratio			
3			
4			
5 Acid-test ratio			
6			
7			
8 Receivables turnover			
9			
10			
11 Inventory turnover			
12			
13			
14 Liquidity analysis			
15			
16			
17 PROFITABILITY			
18 Profit Margin			
19			
20			
21 Asset turnover			
22			
23			
24 Return on assets			
25			
26			
27 Earnings per share			
28			
29			
30 Profitability analysis:			
31			
32			

(b)

MEXICALLI COMPANY Ratio Analysis			
	2003	2004	Change
Return on common			
stockholders' equity			
Debt to total assets			
Price-earnings ratio			

(a)

	Kmart	Wal-Mart
(1) Current ratio		
(2) Receivables turnover		
(3) Inventory turnonver		
(4) Profit margin on sales		
(5) Asset turnover		
(6) Return on assets		
(7) Return on common stockholders' equity		
(8) Debt to total assets		

(a) (Continued)

	Kmart	Wal-Mart
(9) Times interest earned		
(10) Current cash debt coverage		
(11) Cash return on sales		
(12) Cash debt coverage		

(b)

Name

Section

Date

1	(a) Current ratio
2	
3	
4	
5	
6	(b) Acid-test ratio
7	
8	
9	
10	
11	(c) Receivables turnover
12	
13	
14	
15	
16	(d) Inventory turnover
17	
18	
19	
20	
21	(e) Profit margin on sales
22	
23	
24	
25	
26	(f) Asset turnover
27	
28	
29	
30	
31	
32	

1	(g) Return on assets
2	
3	
4	
5	
6	(h) Return on common stockholders' equity
7	
8	
9	
10	(i) Earnings per share
11	
12	
13	
14	
15	(j) Price-earnings ratio
16	
17	
18	
19	(k) Payout ratio
20	
21	
22	
23	
24	(l) Debt to total assets
25	
26	
27	
28	
29	(m) Times interest earned
30	
31	
32	

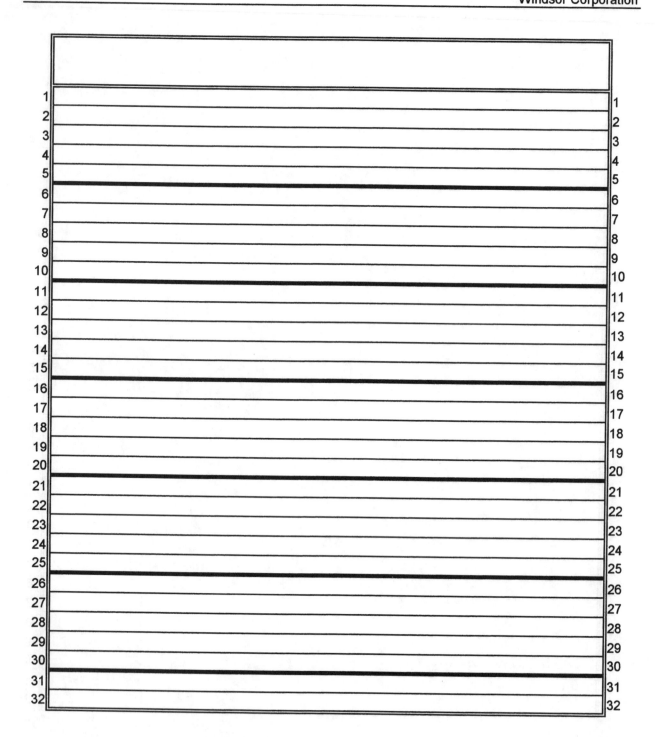

Name

Section

Date

WINDSOR CORPORATION
Income Statement
For the Year Ended December 31, 2003

1		
2	Sales	11 0 0 0 0 0 0
3	Cost of goods sold	
4	Gross profit	
5	Operating expenses	1 6 6 5 0 0 0
6	Income from operations	
7	Other expenses and losses	
8	Interest expense	
9	Income before taxes	
10	Income tax expense	5 6 0 0 0 0
11	Net income	

WINDSOR CORPORATION
Balance Sheet
December 31, 2003

1	ASSETS	
2	Current Assets	
3	Cash	4 5 0 0 0 0
4	Accounts receivable (net)	
5	Inventory	
6	Total current assets	
7	Plant assets (net)	4 6 2 0 0 0 0
8	Total assets	
9		
10	LIABILITIES AND STOCKHOLDERS' EQUITY	
11	Current liabilities	
12	Long-term notes payable	
13	Total liabilities	
14	Common stock, $1 par	3 0 0 0 0 0 0
15	Retained earnings	4 0 0 0 0 0
16	Total stockholders' equity	3 4 0 0 0 0 0
17	Total liabilities and stockholders' equity	

237

(a)

LANDS' END, INC. Trend Analysis of Net Sales and Operating Income For the Fiver Years Ended December 31, 2000					
	2000	1999	1998	1997	1996
(1) Net sales- Amount					
Trend					
(2) Operating income					
Trend					
Analysis:					

(b)

LANDS' END, INC. 2000 and 1999 Ratio Analysis: Profitability		
	2000	1999
(1) Profit margin		
(2) Asset turnover		
(3) Return on assets		
(4) Return on common stockholders' equity		

(b) (Continued)

1	Analysis:	1
2		2
3		3
4		4

(c)

	LANDS' END, INC. 2000 and 1999 Ratio Analysis: Solvency			
		2000	1999	
1	(1) Debt to total assets			1
2				2
3				3
4				4
5	(2) Times interest earned			5
6				6
7				7
8				8
9	Analysis:			9
10				10
11				11

(d)

1		1
2		2
3		3
4		4
5		5
6		6
7		7

	Lands' End	Abercrombie & Fitch
(a)		
(1). Percentage increase (decrease) in net sales		
Percentage increase (decrease) in net income		
(2) Percentage increase (decrease) in total assets		
Percentage increase (decrease) in total stockholders' equity		
3. Earnings per share		
Price-earnings ratio		
(b)		

(a) Liquidity

	Railtrack Group	Burlington Northern
1. Current ratio		
2. Acid-test ratio		
3. Current cash debt coverage		
4. Receivables turnover		
Analysis:		

(b) Solvency

1. Debt to total assets

2. Times interest earned

(b) Continued

	Railtrack Group	Burlington Northern
1. 3. Cash debt coverage		
2.		
3.		
4.		
5. Analysis:		
6.		
7.		
8.		
9.		
10.		
11. (c) Profitability		
12. 1. Asset turnover		
13.		
14.		
15.		
16. 2. Profit margin		
17.		
18.		
19.		
20. 3. Return on assets		
21.		
22.		
23.		
24. 4. Return on common		
25. stockholders' equity		
26.		
27.		
28.		
29. Analysis:		
30.		
31.		
32.		

(c) Continued

1	Analysis (Continued):
2	
3	
4	
5	
6	
7	(d)
8	
9	
10	
11	
12	
13	
14	
15	
16	
17	
18	
19	
20	
21	
22	
23	
24	
25	
26	
27	
28	
29	
30	
31	
32	

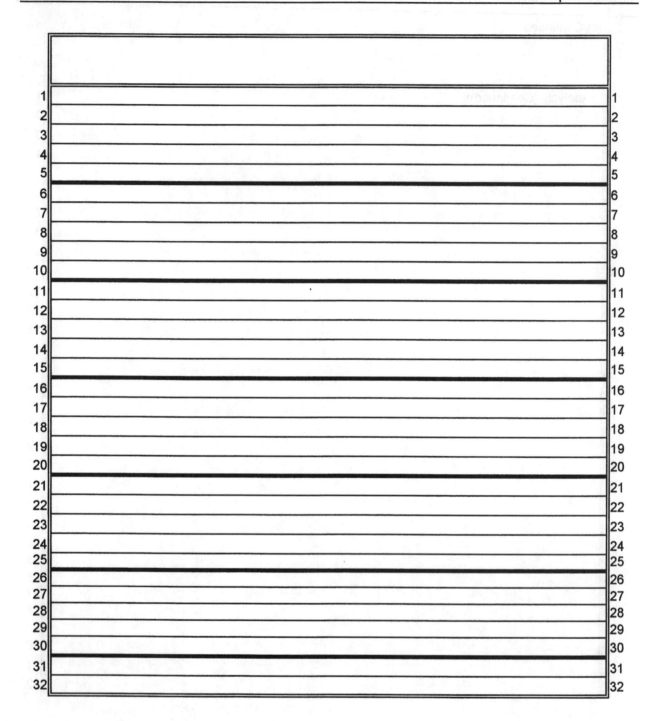

1	1
2	2
3	3
4	4
5	5
6	6
7	7
8	8
9	9
10	10
11	11
12	12
13	13
14	14
15	15
16	16
17	17
18	18
19	19
20	20
21	21
22	22
23	23
24	24
25	25
26	26
27	27
28	28
29	29
30	30
31	31
32	32

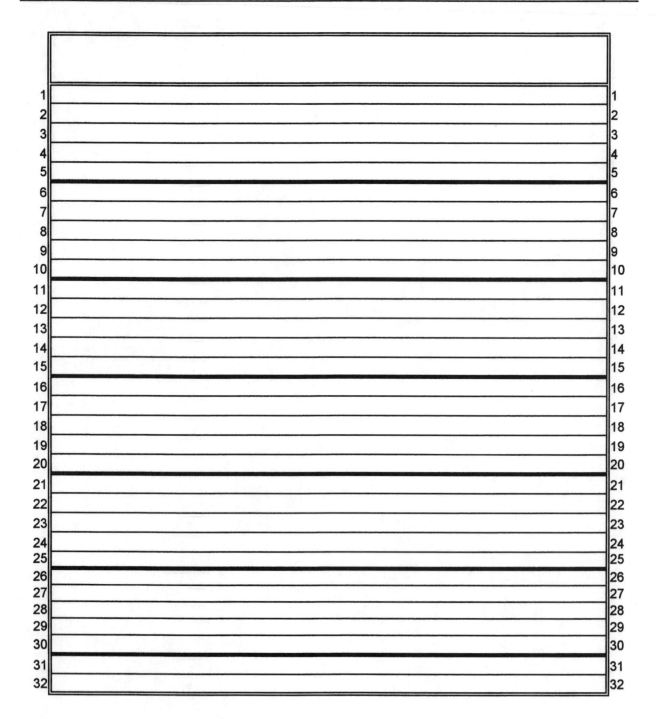

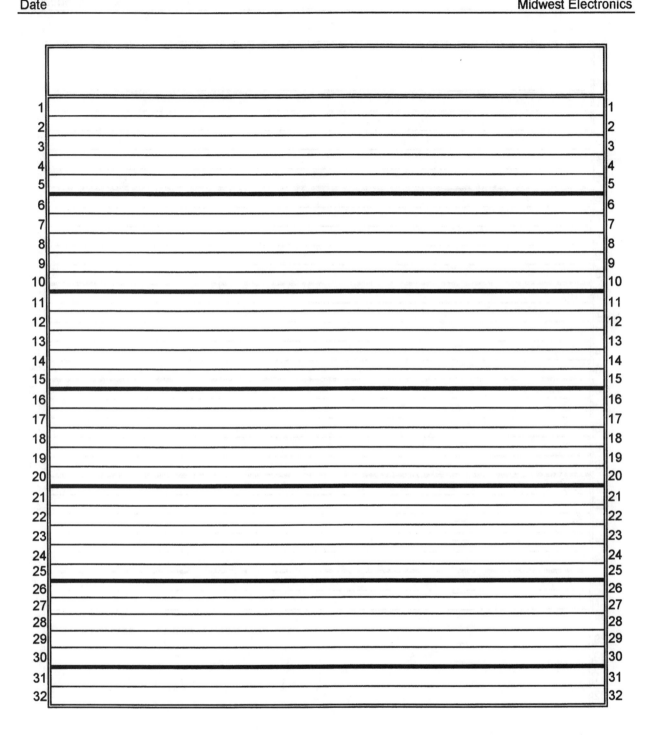

(a)

(b)

(c)

1			1
2			2
3			3
4			4
5			5
6			6
7			7
8			8
9			9
10			10
11			11
12			12
13			13
14			14
15			15
16			16
17			17
18			18
19			19
20			20
21			21
22			22
23			23
24			24
25			25
26			26
27			27
28			28
29			29
30			30
31			31
32			32
33			33
34			34
35			35
36			36
37			37
38			38
39			39
40			40

Name

Section

Date

1						1
2						2
3						3
4						4
5						5
6						6
7						7
8						8
9						9
10						10
11						11
12						12
13						13
14						14
15						15
16						16
17						17
18						18
19						19
20						20
21						21
22						22
23						23
24						24
25						25
26						26
27						27
28						28
29						29
30						30
31						31
32						32
33						33
34						34
35						35
36						36
37						37
38						38
39						39
40						40

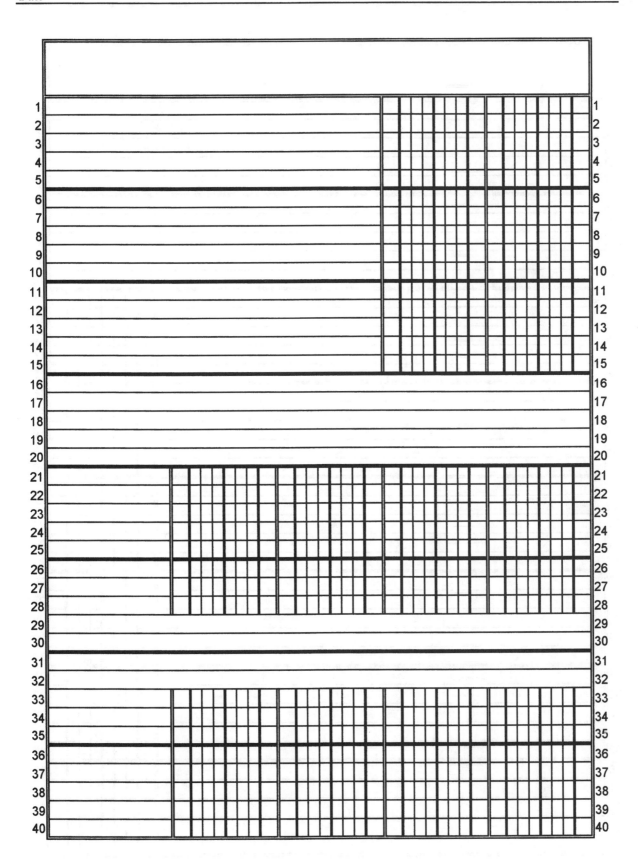

#1		

#2

#3

1		1
2		2
3		3
4		4
5		5
6		6
7		7
8		8
9		9
10		10

#4

11		11
12		12
13		13
14		14
15		15
16		16
17		17
18		18
19		19
20		20
21		21
22		22
23		23
24		24
25		25
26		26
27		27
28		28
29		29
30		30
31		31
32		32
33		33
34		34
35		35
36		36
37		37
38		38
39		39
40		40

1	CASE A:	1
2		2
3		3
4		4
5		5
6		6
7		7
8		8
9		9
10		10
11		11
12		12
13		13
14	CASE B:	14
15		15
16		16
17		17
18		18
19		19
20		20
21		21
22		22
23		23
24		24
25		25
26		26
27	CASE C:	27
28		28
29		29
30		30
31		31
32		32
33		33
34		34
35		35
36		36
37		37
38		38
39		39
40		40

(a)

1					1
2					2
3					3
4					4
5					5
6					6
7					7
8					8
9					9
10					10
11					11
12					12
13					13
14					14
15					15
16					16
17					17
18					18
19					19
20					20
21					21
22					22
23					23
24					24

(b)

HOLLIS COMPANY

Cost of Goods Manufactured Schedule

For The Year Ended December 31, 2002

1		1
2		2
3		3
4		4
5		5
6		6
7		7
8		8
9		9
10		10

(a)

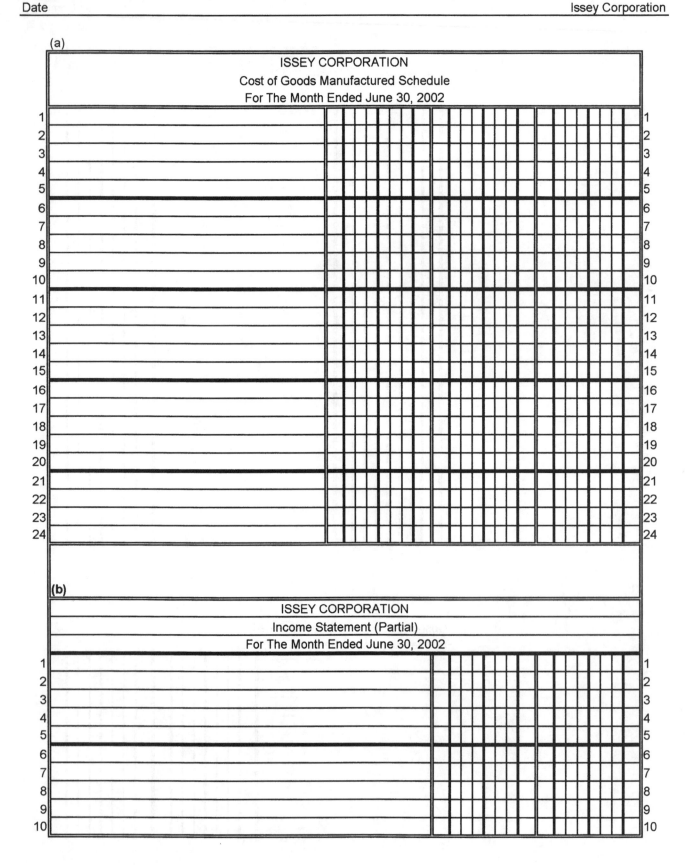

ISSEY CORPORATION

Cost of Goods Manufactured Schedule

For The Month Ended June 30, 2002

(b)

ISSEY CORPORATION

Income Statement (Partial)

For The Month Ended June 30, 2002

Name

Section

Date

#8

1		1
2		2
3		3
4		4
5		5
6		6
7		7
8		8
9		9
10		10
11		11
12		12
13		13
14		14
15		15
16		16
17		17
18	#10	18
19		19
20		20
21		21
22		22
23		23
24		24
25		25
26		26
27		27
28		28
29		29
30		30
31		31
32		32
33		33
34		34
35		35
36		36
37		37
38		38
39		39
40		40

(a)

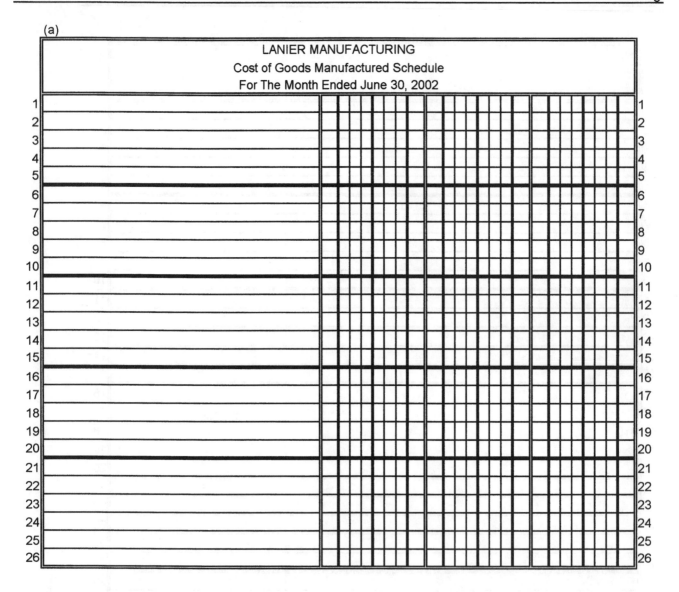

LANIER MANUFACTURING

Cost of Goods Manufactured Schedule

For The Month Ended June 30, 2002

(b)

LANIER MANUFACTURING

(Partial) Balance Sheet

June 30, 2002

(a)

CASE 1

CASE 2

(b)

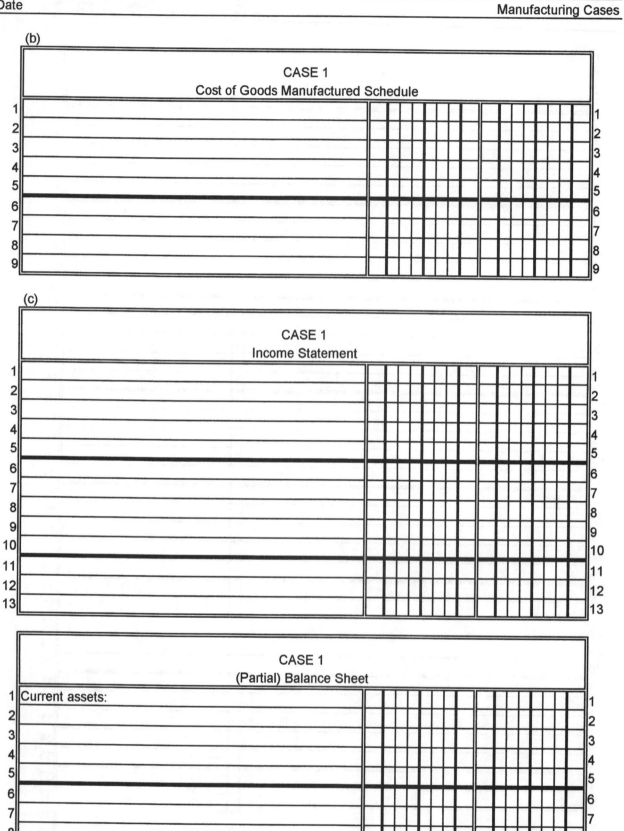

CASE 1
Cost of Goods Manufactured Schedule

(c)

CASE 1
Income Statement

CASE 1
(Partial) Balance Sheet

Current assets:

(a)

	ISTANBUL COMPANY					
	Cost of Goods Manufactured Schedule					
	For The Month Ended October 31, 2002					

(b)

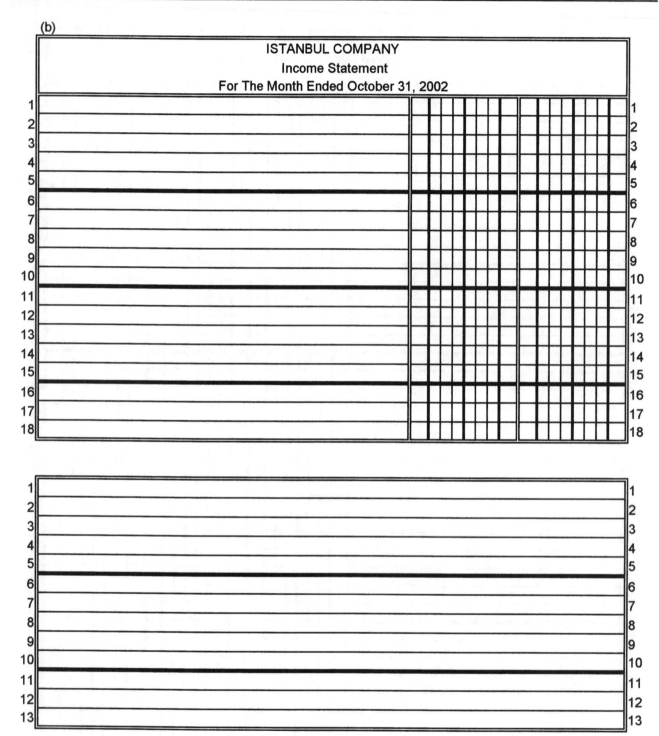

ISTANBUL COMPANY
Income Statement
For The Month Ended October 31, 2002

Name _____

Section _____

Date _____

Kanjo Company

(a)

Cost Item	Products Costs			Period Costs	Prime Costs	Conversion Costs
	Direct Materials	Direct Labor	Manufacturing Overhead			
1 Maintenance costs on factory building						
2 Factory manager's salary						
3 Advertising for motorcycles						
4 Sales commissions						
5 Depreciation on factory building						
6 Rent on factory equipment						
7 Insurance on factory building						
8 Raw materials						
9 Utility costs for factory						
10 Supplies for general office						
11 Wages for assembly workers						
12 Depreciation on office equipment						
13 Miscellaneous materials						
14						
15						
16						
17						
18						

(b)

19 Total production costs:		
20	Cost to produce one motorcycle:	
21		
22		
23		
24		
25		

Match Company

(a)

Cost Item	Products Costs			Period Costs	Prime Costs	Conversion Costs
	Direct Materials	Direct Labor	Manufacturing Overhead			
1						
2						
3						
4						
5						
6						
7						
8						
9						
10						
11						
12						
13						
14						
15						
16						
17						

(b)

Total production costs:

Cost to produce one tennis racket:

18		
19		
20		
21		
22		
23		
24		
25		

(a)

CASE 1

CASE 2

(b)

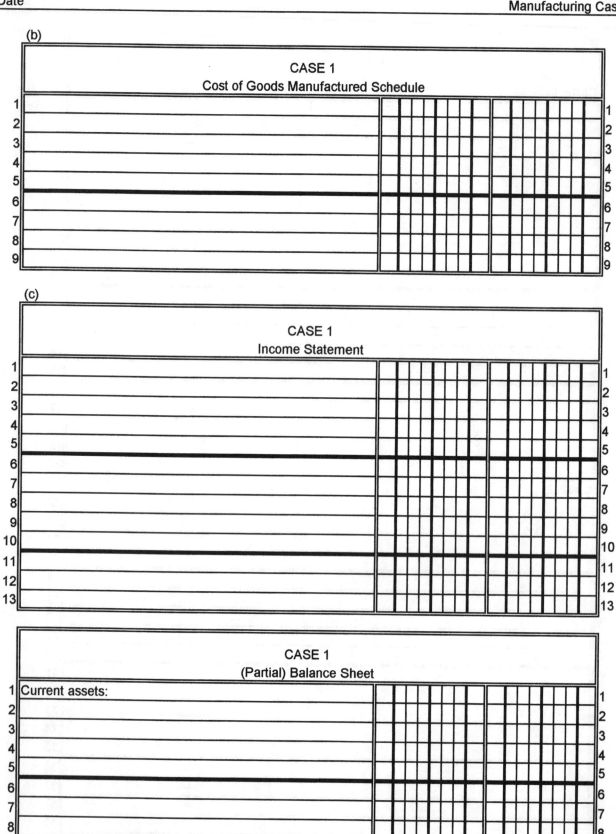

CASE 1
Cost of Goods Manufactured Schedule

(c)

CASE 1
Income Statement

CASE 1
(Partial) Balance Sheet

Current assets:

(a)

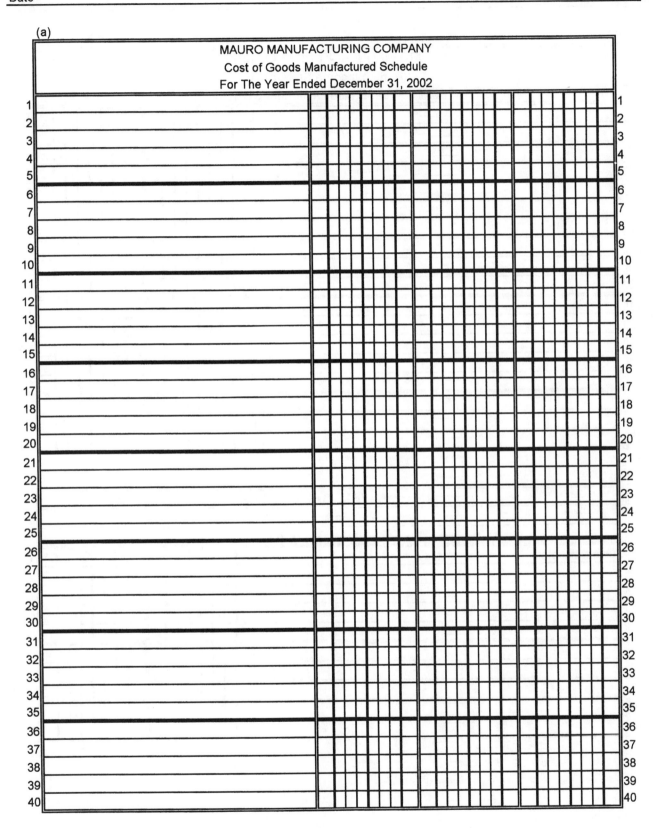

MAURO MANUFACTURING COMPANY
Cost of Goods Manufactured Schedule
For The Year Ended December 31, 2002

(b)

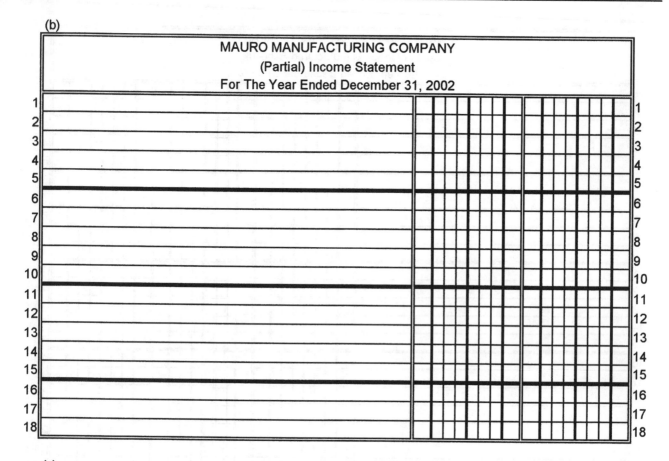

MAURO MANUFACTURING COMPANY
(Partial) Income Statement
For The Year Ended December 31, 2002

(c)

MAURO MANUFACTURING COMPANY
(Partial) Balance Sheet
December 31, 2002

Current assets:

(a)

CHELSEA COMPANY
Cost of Goods Manufactured Schedule
For The Month Ended August 31, 2002

(b)

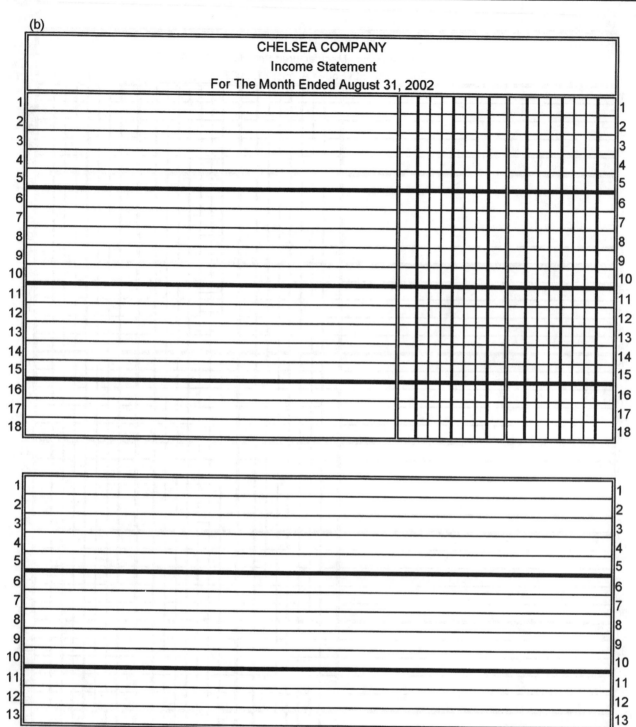

CHELSEA COMPANY
Income Statement
For The Month Ended August 31, 2002

1	Ending Raw Materials Inventory	1
2		2
3		3
4		4
5		5
6		6
7		7
8		8
9		9
10		10
11		11
12		12
13		13
14		14
15	Ending Work In Process Inventory	15
16		16
17		17
18		18
19		19
20		20
21		21
22		22
23		23
24		24
25		25
26		26
27		27
28		28
29		29
30		30
31		31
32		32
33		33
34		34
35		35
36		36
37		37
38		38
39		39
40		40

	1
1	1
2	2
3	3
4	4
5	5
6	6
7	7
8	8
9	9
10	10
11	11
12	12
13	13
14	14
15	15
16 Ending Finished Goods Inventory	16
17	17
18	18
19	19
20	20
21	21
22	22
23	23
24	24
25	25
26	26
27	27
28	28
29	29
30	30
31	31
32	32
33	33
34	34
35	35
36	36
37	37
38	38
39	39
40	40

(a)

1	1
2	2
3	3
4	4
5	5
6	6
7	7
8	8
9	9
10	10
11	11
12	12
13	13
14	14

(b)

15	15
16	16
17	17
18	18
19	19
20	20
21	21
22	22
23	23
24	24
25	25

(c)

26	26
27	27
28	28
29	29
30	30
31	31
32	32
33	33
34	34
35	35
36	36
37	37
38	38
39	39
40	40

	1
1	
2	2
3	3
4	4
5	5
6	6
7	7
8	8
9	9
10	10
11	11
12	12
13	13
14	14
15	15
16	16
17	17
18	18
19	19
20	20
21	21
22	22
23	23
24	24
25	25
26	26
27	27
28	28
29	29
30	30
31	31
32	32
33	33
34	34
35	35
36	36
37	37
38	38
39	39
40	40

1	1
2	2
3	3
4	4
5	5
6	6
7	7
8	8
9	9
10	10
11	11
12	12
13	13
14	14
15	15
16	16
17	17
18	18
19	19
20	20
21	21
22	22
23	23
24	24
25	25
26	26
27	27
28	28
29	29
30	30
31	31
32	32
33	33
34	34
35	35
36	36
37	37
38	38
39	39
40	40

1	1
2	2
3	3
4	4
5	5
6	6
7	7
8	8
9	9
10	10
11	11
12	12
13	13
14	14
15	15
16	16
17	17
18	18
19	19
20	20
21	21
22	22
23	23
24	24
25	25
26	26
27	27
28	28
29	29
30	30
31	31
32	32
33	33
34	34
35	35
36	36
37	37
38	38
39	39
40	40

	1				1
1					
2					2
3					3
4					4
5					5
6					6
7					7
8					8
9					9
10					10
11					11
12					12
13					13
14					14
15					15
16					16
17					17
18					18
19					19
20					20
21					21
22					22
23					23
24					24
25					25
26					26
27					27
28					28
29					29
30					30
31					31
32					32
33					33
34					34
35					35
36					36
37					37
38					38
39					39
40					40

1	1
2	2
3	3
4	4
5	5
6	6
7	7
8	8
9	9
10	10
11	11
12	12
13	13
14	14
15	15
16	16
17	17
18	18
19	19
20	20
21	21
22	22
23	23
24	24
25	25
26	26
27	27
28	28
29	29
30	30
31	31
32	32
33	33
34	34
35	35
36	36
37	37
38	38
39	39
40	40

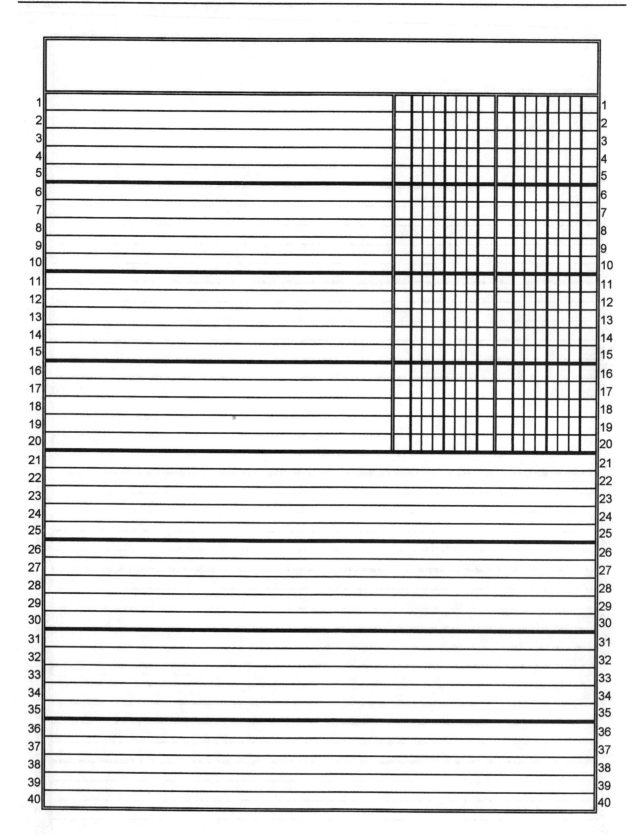

Name

Section

Date

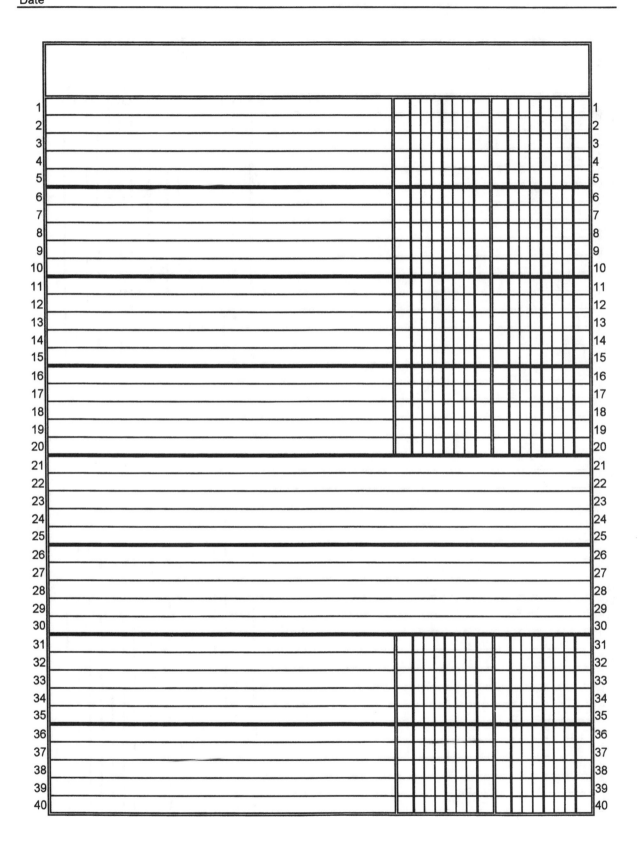

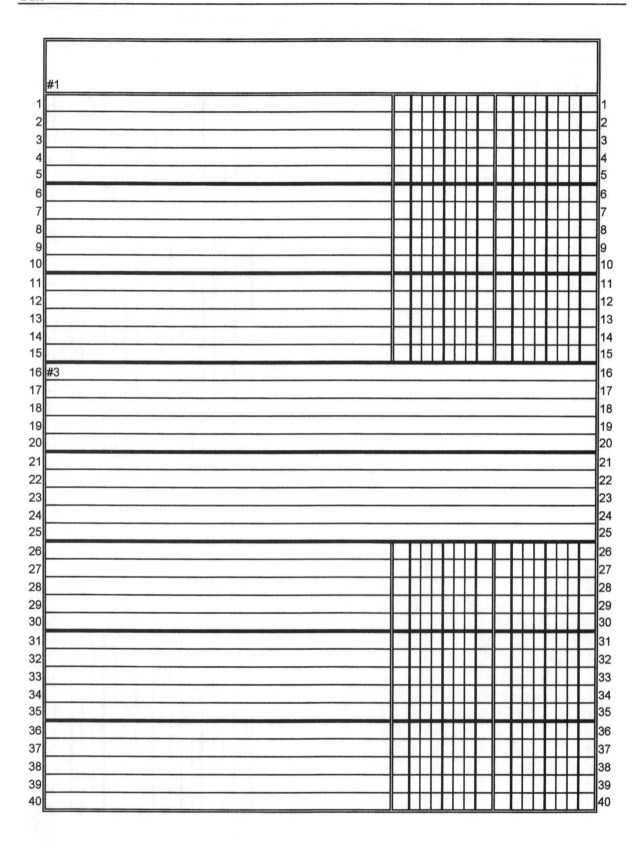

#5

#6

CASE C:

General Journal

Trans-action	Account Titles and Explanation	Debit	Credit
1			
2			
3			
4			
5			
6			
7			
8			
9			
10			
11			
12			
13			
14			
15			
16			
17			
18			
19			
20			
21			
22			
23			
24			
25			
26			
27			
28			
29			
30			
31			
32			
33			
34			
35			
36			
37			
38			
39			
40			

(a)

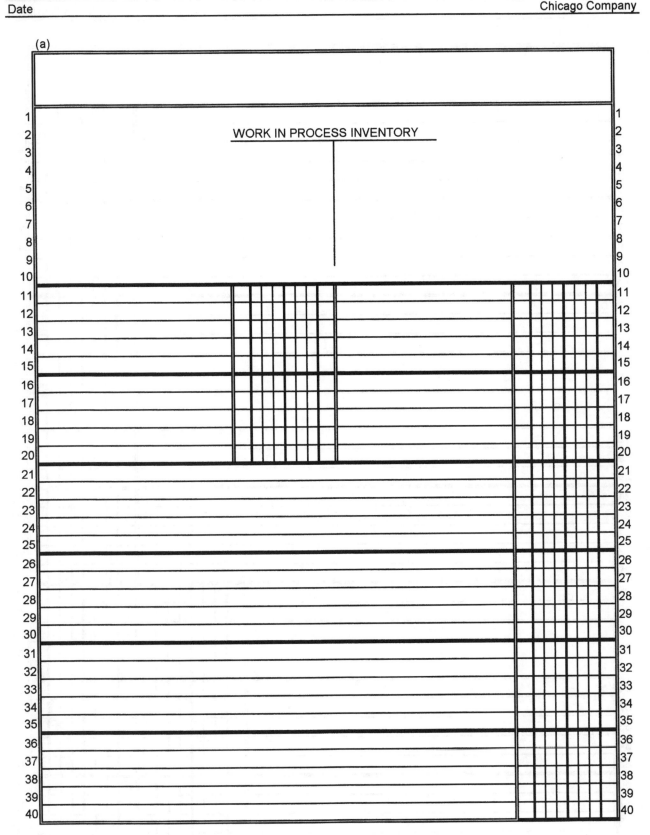

WORK IN PROCESS INVENTORY

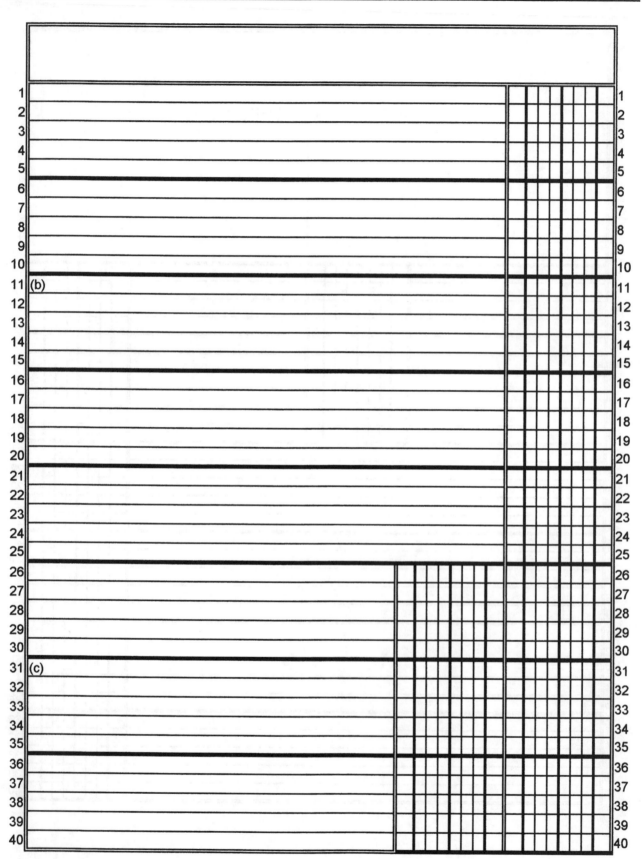

(b)

(c)

(c), (d), (e) Continued, and (f)

	Account Titles and Explanation	Debit	Credit	
1	(c)			1
2				2
3				3
4				4
5				5
6				6
7				7
8				8
9				9
10				10
11				11
12				12
13				13
14				14
15	(d)			15
16				16
17				17
18				18
19				19
20				20
21				21
22				22
23				23
24				24
25				25
26				26
27				27
28	(e)			28
29				29
30				30
31				31
32				32
33	(f)			33
34				34
35				35
36				36
37				37
38				38
39				39
40				40

(g)

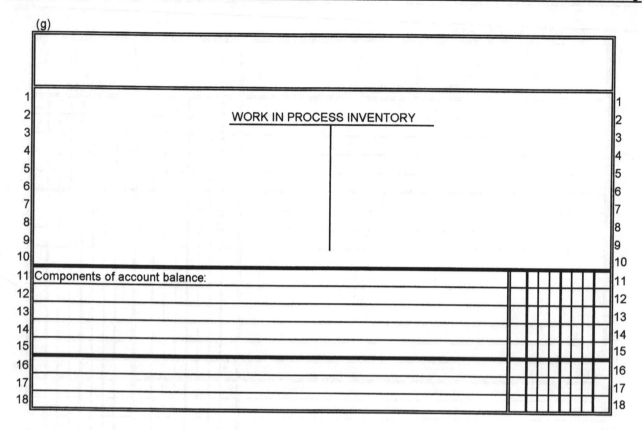

WORK IN PROCESS INVENTORY

Components of account balance:

(h)

MANUFACTURING OVERHEAD

(a)

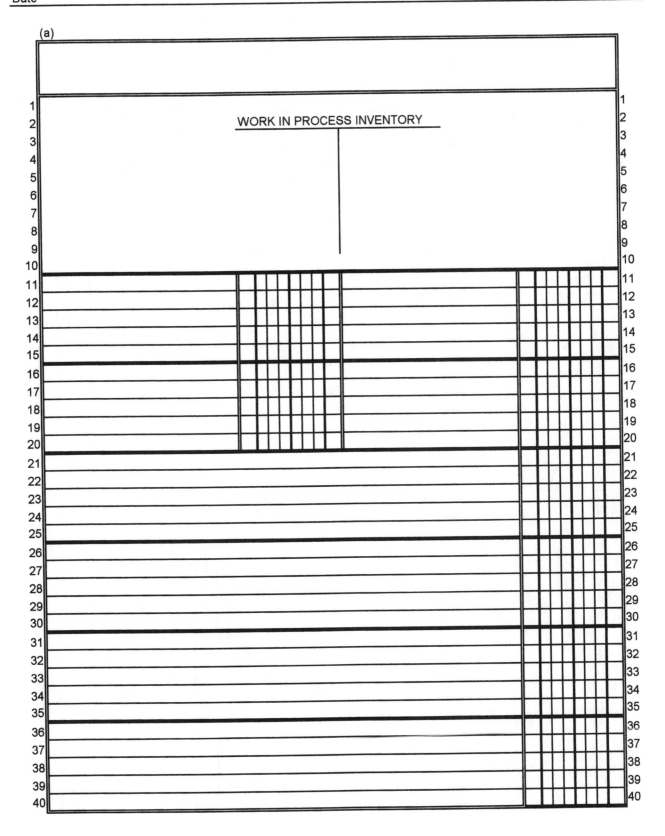

WORK IN PROCESS INVENTORY

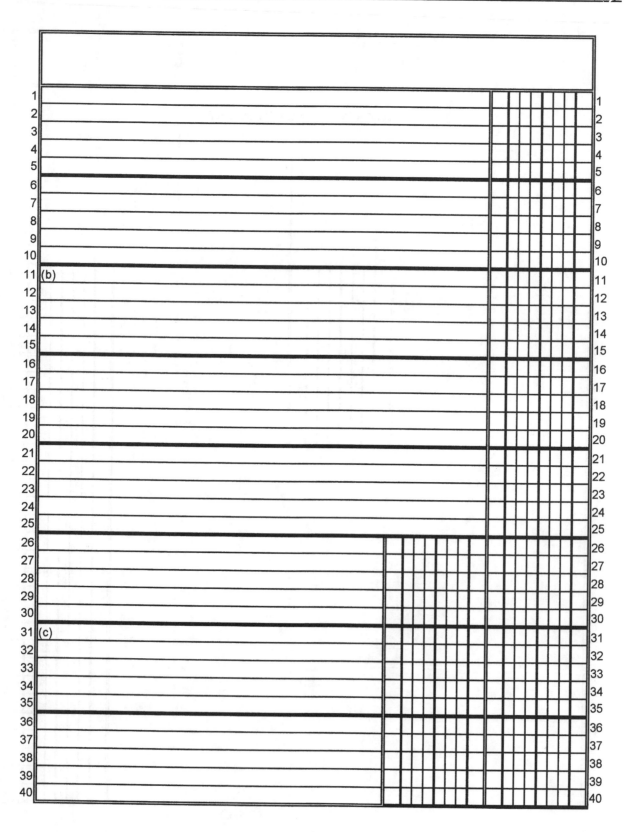

(b)

(c)

(a)

Account Titles and Explanations	Debit	Credit
1		
2		
3		
4		
5		
6		
7		
8		
9		
10		
11		
12		
13		
14		
15		
16		
17		
18		
19		
20		
21		
22		
23		
24		
25		
26		
27		
28		
29		
30		

Job	Beginning Work-in Process	Direct Materials	Direct Labor	Manufacturing Overhead	Total Cost
1					
2					
3					
4					
5					

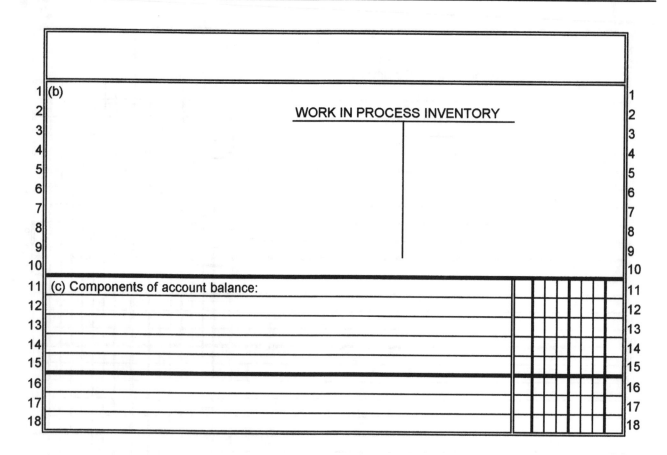

(b)

WORK IN PROCESS INVENTORY

(c) Components of account balance:

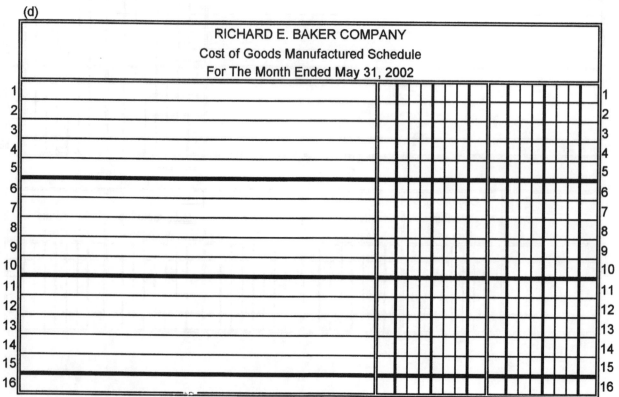

(d)

RICHARD E. BAKER COMPANY

Cost of Goods Manufactured Schedule

For The Month Ended May 31, 2002

(a), (d), and (e)

1 (a)	1
2	2
3	3
4	4
5	5
6	6
7	7
8	8
9 (d)	9
10	10
11	11
12	12
13 (e)	13
14	14
15	15
16	16

(b)

Manufacturing Costs	Department			
	A	B	C	
1				1
2				2
3				3
4				4
5				5
6				6

(c)

Manufacturing Costs	Department			
	A	B	C	
1				1
2				2
3				3
4				4
5				5
6				6

(a) - (g)

	1							1
2								2
3								3
4								4
5								5
6								6
7								7
8								8
9								9
10								10
11								11
12								12
13								13
14								14
15								15
16								16
17								17
18								18
19								19
20								20
21								21
22								22
23								23
24								24
25								25
26								26
27								27
28								28
29								29
30								30
31								31
32								32
33								33
34								34
35								35
36								36
37								37
38								38
39								39
40								40

(h) - (n)

1	1
2	2
3	3
4	4
5	5
6	6
7	7
8	8
9	9
10	10
11	11
12	12
13	13
14	14
15	15
16	16
17	17
18	18
19	19
20	20
21	21
22	22
23	23
24	24
25	25
26	26
27	27
28	28
29	29
30	30
31	31
32	32
33	33
34	34
35	35
36	36
37	37
38	38
39	39
40	40

(a) and (b)

(c)

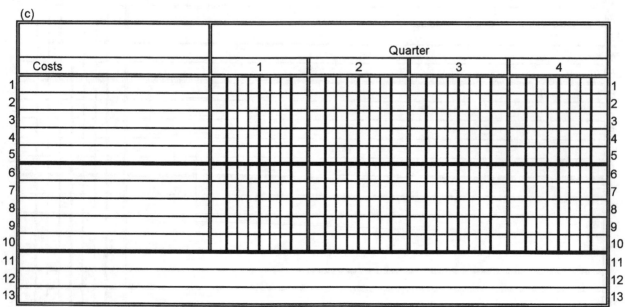

1	FIRST ENTRY	1
2	(a)	2
3		3
4		4
5		5
6	(b)	6
7		7
8		8
9		9
10		10
11	SECOND ENTRY	11
12	(a)	12
13		13
14		14
15		15
16	(b)	16
17		17
18		18
19		19
20		20
21	THIRD ENTRY	21
22	(a)	22
23		23
24		24
25		25
26	(b)	26
27		27
28		28
29		29
30		30
31	FOURTH ENTRY	31
32	(a)	32
33		33
34		34
35		35
36	(b)	36
37		37
38		38
39		39
40		40

1	1
2	2
3	3
4	4
5	5
6	6
7	7
8	8
9	9
10	10
11	11
12	12
13	13
14	14
15	15
16	16
17	17
18	18
19	19
20	20
21	21
22	22
23	23
24	24
25	25
26	26
27	27
28	28
29	29
30	30
31	31
32	32
33	33
34	34
35	35
36	36
37	37
38	38
39	39
40	40

1
2
3
4
5
6
7
8
9
10
11
12
13
14
15
16
17
18
19
20
21
22
23
24
25
26
27
28
29
30
31
32
33
34
35
36
37
38
39
40

1
2
3
4
5
6
7
8
9
10
11
12
13
14
15
16
17
18
19
20
21
22
23
24
25
26
27
28
29
30
31
32
33
34
35
36
37
38
39
40

	Date	Account Titles and Explanation	Debit	Credit	
1					1
2					2
3					3
4					4
5					5
6					6
7					7
8					8
9					9
10					10
11					11
12					12
13					13
14					14
15					15
16					16
17					17
18					18
19					19
20					20
21					21
22					22
23					23
24					24
25					25
26					26
27					27
28					28
29					29
30					30
31					31
32					32
33					33
34					34
35					35
36					36
37					37
38					38
39					39
40					40

Name

Section

Date

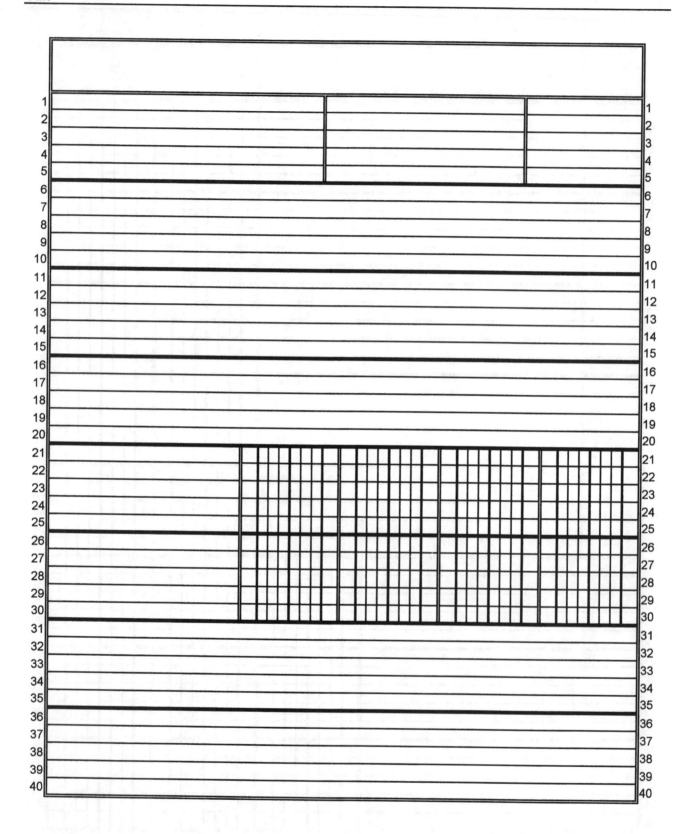

		1
1		2
2		3
3		4
4		5
5		6
6		7
7		8
8		9
9		10
10		11
11		12
12		13
13		14
14		15
15		16
16		17
17		18
18		19
19		20
20		21
21		22
22		23
23		24
24		25
25		26
26		27
27		28
28		29
29		30
30		31
31		32
32		33
33		34
34		35
35		36
36		37
37		38
38		39
39		40
40		

#1

1				1
2				2
3				3
4				4
5				5
6				6
7				7
8				8
9				9
10				10
11				11
12				12
13				13
14				14
15				15
16				16
17				17
18				18
19				19
20				20

#2

21				21
22				22
23				23
24				24
25				25
26				26
27				27
28				28
29				29
30				30
31				31
32				32
33				33
34				34
35				35
36				36
37				37
38				38
39				39
40				40

	COPA FURNITURE			
	Sanding Department			
	For The Month Ended March 31, 2002			
		Equivalent Units		
	Physical Units	Materials	Conversion Costs	Total
1				
2				
3				
4				
5				
6				
7				
8				
9				
10				
11				
12				
13				
14				
15				
16				
17				
18				
19				
20				
21				
22				
23				
24				
25				
26				
27				
28				
29				
30				
31				
32				
33				
34				
35				
36				
37				

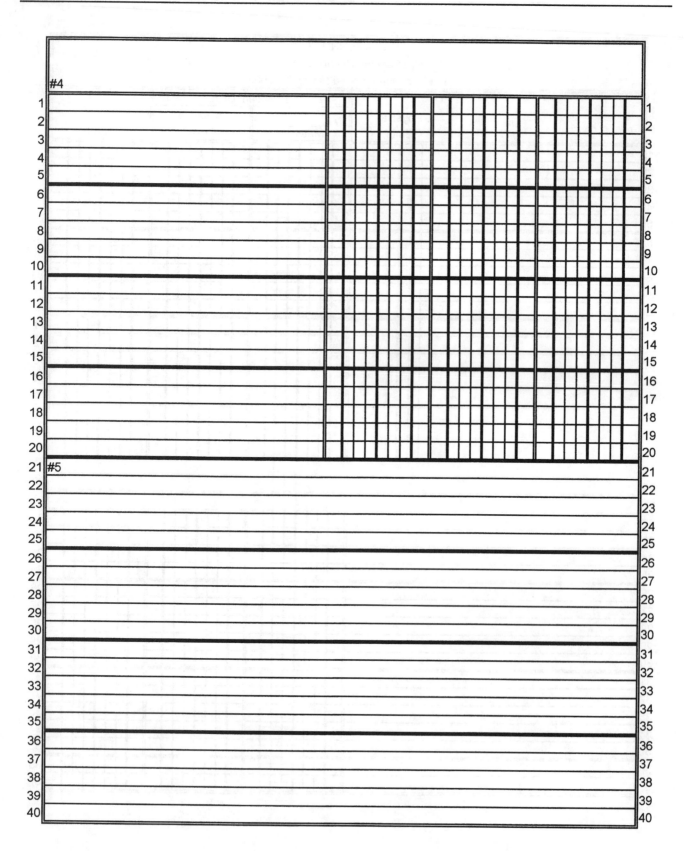

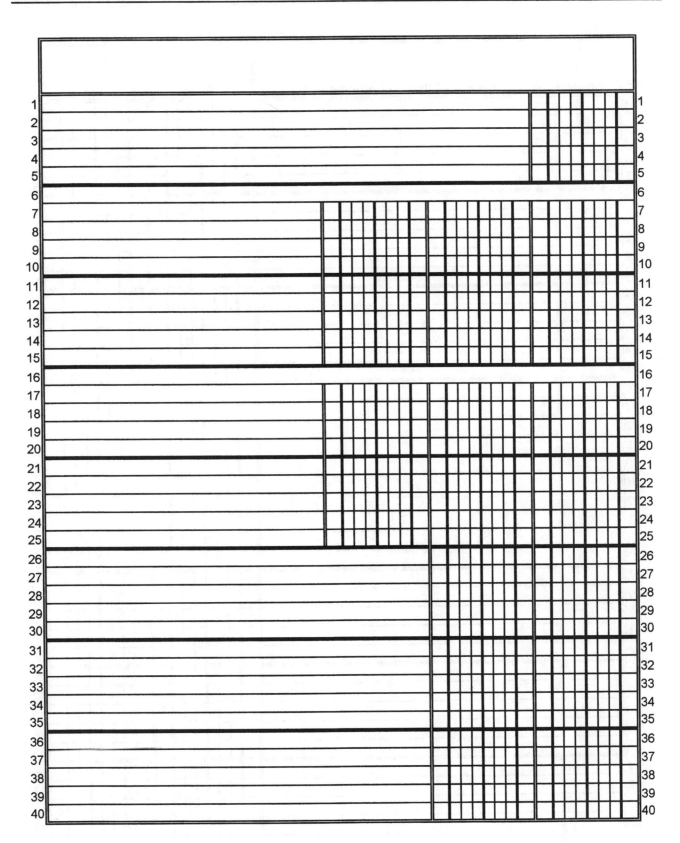

Trans-action Number	Account Titles and Explanation	Debit	Credit	
1				1
2				2
3				3
4				4
5				5
6				6
7				7
8				8
9				9
10				10
11				11
12				12
13				13
14				14
15				15
16				16
17				17
18				18
19				19
20				20
21				21
22				22
23				23
24				24
25				25
26				26
27				27
28				28
29				29
30				30
31				31
32				32
33				33
34				34
35				35
36				36
37				37
38				38
39				39
40				40

| | Physical Units | Equivalent Units | | Total |
		Materials	Conversion Costs	
1				
2				
3				
4				
5				
6				
7				
8				
9				
10				
11				
12				
13				
14				
15				
16				
17				
18				
19				
20				
21				
22				
23				
24				
25				
26				
27				
28				
29				
30				
31				
32				
33				
34				
35				
36				
37				
38				
39				
40				

		Equivalent Units		
	Physical Units	Materials	Conversion Costs	Total
1				
2				
3				
4				
5				
6				
7				
8				
9				
10				
11				
12				
13				
14				
15				
16				
17				
18				
19				
20				
21				
22				
23				
24				
25				
26				
27				
28				
29				
30				
31				
32				
33				
34				
35				
36				

TOMLIN MANUFACTURING COMPANY
Welding Department
Production Cost Report
For The Month Ended February 28, 2002

Name

Section

Date

	Date	Account Titles and Explanation	Debit	Credit	
1					1
2					2
3					3
4					4
5					5
6					6
7					7
8					8
9					9
10					10
11					11
12					12
13					13
14					14
15					15
16					16
17					17
18					18
19					19
20					20
21					21
22					22
23					23
24					24
25					25
26					26
27					27
28					28
29					29
30					30
31					31
32					32
33					33
34					34
35					35
36					36
37					37
38					38
39					39
40					40

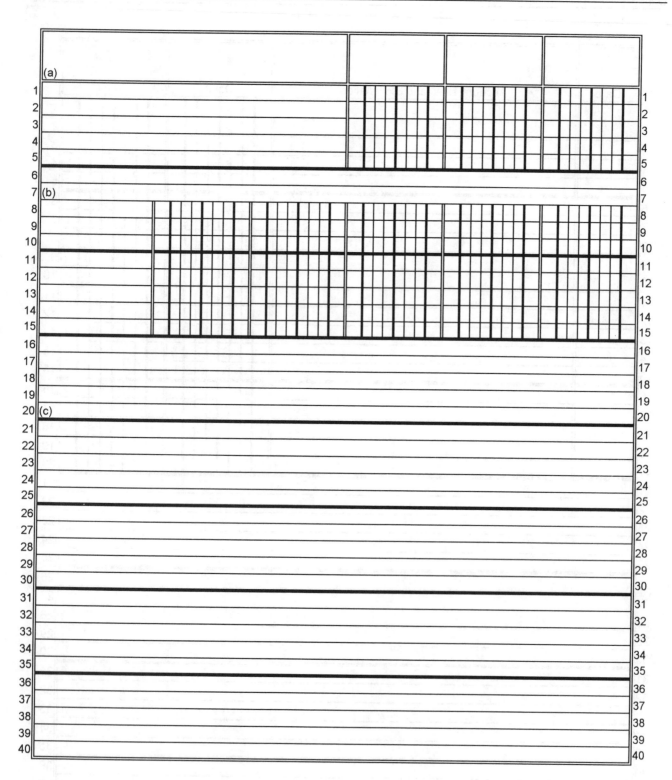

(a)	Physical Units	Equivalent Units	
		Materials	Conversion Costs
1 Units to be accounted for:			
2			
3			
4			
5			
6			
7 Units accounted for:			
8			
9			
10			
11			
12 Costs:			
13			
14			
15			
16			
17			
18 Cost per unit			
19			
20			
21 Costs accounted for:			
22			
23			
24			
25			
26			
27			
28			
29			
30			
31			
32			
33			
34			
35			
36			
37			
38			
39			
40			

(b)

	SPRAGUE COMPANY Basketball Department Production Cost Report For The Month Ended July 31, 2002			
	Physical Units	Equivalent Units		Total
		Materials	Conversion Costs	
1 Quantities:				
2 Units to be accounted for				
3				
4				
5				
6				
7 Units accounted for				
8				
9				
10				
11				
12 Costs:				
13 Unit costs:				
14				
15				
16				
17				
18 Costs to be accounted for				
19				
20				
21				
22				
23				
24 Costs accounted for				
25				
26				
27				
28				
29				
30				
31				
32				
33				
34				
35				
36				

	Physical Units	Equivalent Units	
		Materials	Conversion Costs
(a) Computation of equivalent units:			
Computation of October unit costs:			
(b) Cost Reconciliation Schedule:			

(a)

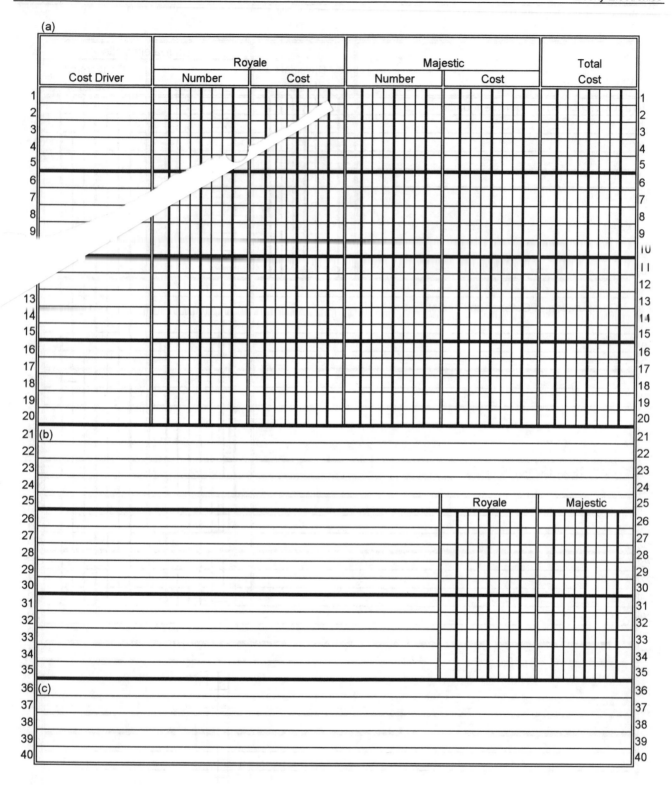

	Cost Driver	Royale		Majestic		Total
		Number	Cost	Number	Cost	Cost
1						
2						
3						
4						
5						
6						
7						
8						
9						

(b)

	Royale	Majestic

(c)

(a)

1 Physical units:
2
3
4
5
6
7
8
9
10

11 (b) Equivalent units:
12

		Materials	Conversion Costs

13
14
15
16
17
18
19
20

21 (c) Unit costs:
22

		Materials	Conversion Costs	Total

23
24
25
26
27
28
29

30 (d) Costs accounted for:
31

		Equivalent Units	Unit Costs	Total Costs Assigned

32
33
34
35
36
37
38
39
40

(e)

			Molding Department Production Cost Report For The Month Ended January 31, 2002		
			Physical Units	Equivalent Units	
				Materials	Conversion Costs	Total
1	Quantities:					
2	Units to be accounted for					
3						
4						
5						
6						
7	Units accounted for					
8						
9						
10						
11						
12	Costs:					
13	Unit costs:					
14						
15						
16						
17						
18	Costs to be accounted for					
19						
20						
21						
22						
23						
24	Costs accounted for					
25						
26						
27						
28						
29						
30						
31						
32						
33						
34						
35						
36						
37						

(a)

	R12 Refrigerators	F24 Freezers
(1) Physical units:		

(2) Equivalent units:

	R12 Refrigerators	
		Conversion
	Materials	Costs

	F24 Freezers	
		Conversion
	Materials	Costs

(3) Unit costs:

	R12 Refrigerators	F24 Freezers

(a) Continued

(4)

	R12 Refrigerators
Costs accounted for:	

	F24 Freezers
Costs accounted for:	

(b)

	Stamping Department - Plant A Production Cost Report For The Month Ended June 30, 2002			
	Physical Units	Equivalent Units		Total
		Materials	Conversion Costs	
Quantities:				
Units to be accounted for				
Units accounted for				
Costs:				
Unit costs:				
Costs to be accounted for				
Costs accounted for				

Trans-action	Account Titles and Explanation	Debit	Credit	
1				1
2				2
3				3
4				4
5				5
6				6
7				7
8				8
9				9
10				10
11				11
12				12
13				13
14				14
15				15
16				16
17				17
18				18
19				19
20				20
21				21
22				22
23				23
24				24
25				25
26				26
27				27
28				28
29				29
30				30
31				31
32				32
33				33
34				34
35				35
36				36
37				37
38				38
39				39
40				40

	Physical Units	Equivalent Units	
		Materials	Conversion Costs
(a)			
1 Units to be accounted for:			
2			
3			
4			
5			
6			
7 Units accounted for:			
8			
9			
10			
11			
12 Costs:			
13			
14			
15			
16			
17			
18 Cost per unit			
19			
20 (b)			
21 Costs accounted for:			
22			
23			
24			
25			
26			
27			
28			
29			
30			
31			
32			
33			
34			
35			
36			
37			
38			
39			
40			

(c)

WANG COMPANY				
Assembly Department				
Production Cost Report				
For The Month Ended October 31, 2002				

	Physical Units	Equivalent Units		Total
		Materials	Conversion Costs	
1 Quantities:				
2 Units to be accounted for				
3				
4				
5				
6				
7 Units accounted for				
8				
9				
10				
11				
12 Costs:				
13 Unit costs:				
14				
15				
16				
17				
18 Costs to be accounted for				
19				
20				
21				
22				
23				
24 Costs accounted for				
25				
26				
27				
28				
29				
30				
31				
32				
33				
34				
35				
36				

(a)	Physical Units	Equivalent Units		Total
		Materials	Conversion Costs	
1 Units to be accounted for:				
2				
3				
4				
5				
6				
7 Units accounted for:				
8				
9				
10				
11				
12 Costs:				
13				
14				
15				
16				
17				
18 Cost per unit				
19				
20				
21 Costs accounted for:				
22				
23				
24				
25				
26				
27				
28				
29				
30				
31				
32				
33				
34				
35				
36				
37				
38				
39				
40				

(b)

	CLEMENTE COMPANY			
	Bicycle Department			
	Production Cost Report			
	For The Month Ended May 31, 2002			
	Physical Units	Equivalent Units		Total
		Materials	Conversion Costs	
1 Quantities:				
2 Units to be accounted for				
3				
4				
5				
6				
7 Units accounted for				
8				
9				
10				
11				
12 Costs:				
13 Unit costs:				
14				
15				
16				
17				
18 Costs to be accounted for				
19				
20				
21				
22				
23				
24 Costs accounted for				
25				
26				
27				
28				
29				
30				
31				
32				
33				
34				
35				
36				

	Physical Units	Equivalent Units	
		Materials	Conversion Costs
(a) Computation of equivalent units:			
Computation of March unit costs:			
(b) Cost Reconciliation Schedule:			

(a)

(b)

(b)

ENGLISH BAY BEACH COMPANY
Mixing Department
Production Cost Report
For The Month Ended July 31, 2002

	Physical Units	Equivalent Units		Total
		Materials	Conversion Costs	
1 Quantities:				
2 Units to be accounted for				
3				
4				
5				
6				
7 Units accounted for				
8				
9				
10				
11				
12 Costs:				
13 Unit costs:				
14				
15				
16				
17				
18 Costs to be accounted for				
19				
20				
21				
22				
23				
24 Costs accounted for				
25				
26				
27				
28				
29				
30				
31				
32				
33				
34				
35				
36				

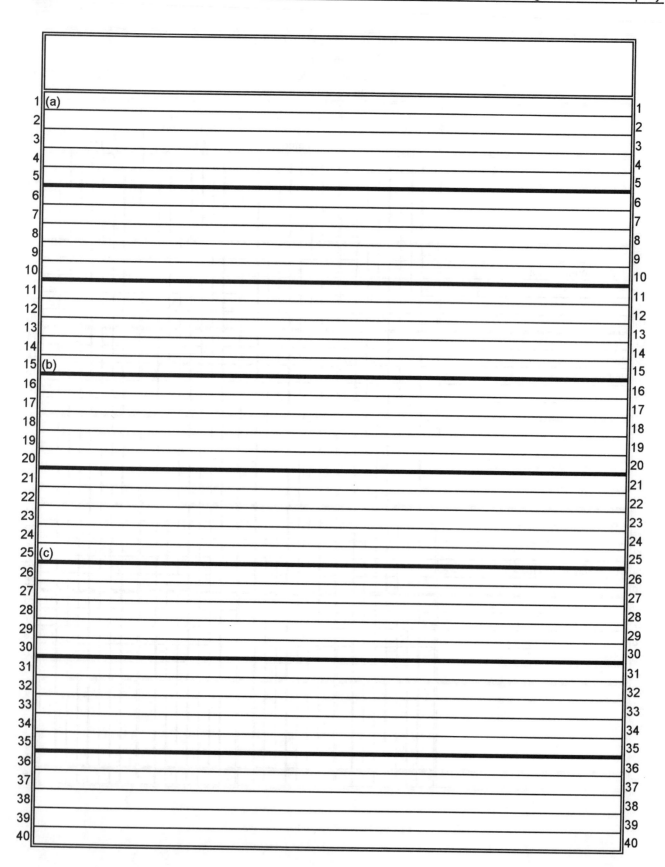

(a)

(b)

(c)

Name

Section

Date

(a)

(b)

(c)

Name

Section

Date

1	1
2	2
3	3
4	4
5	5
6	6
7	7
8	8
9	9
10	10
11	11
12	12
13	13
14	14
15	15
16	16
17	17
18	18
19	19
20	20
21	21
22	22
23	23
24	24
25	25
26	26
27	27
28	28
29	29
30	30
31	31
32	32
33	33
34	34
35	35
36	36
37	37
38	38
39	39
40	40

	1		1
	2		2
	3		3
	4		4
	5		5
	6		6
	7		7
	8		8
	9		9
	10		10
	11		11
	12		12
	13		13
	14		14
	15		15
	16		16
	17		17
	18		18
	19		19
	20		20
	21		21
	22		22
	23		23
	24		24
	25		25
	26		26
	27		27
	28		28
	29		29
	30		30
	31		31
	32		32
	33		33
	34		34
	35		35
	36		36
	37		37
	38		38
	39		39
	40		40

1	1
2	2
3	3
4	4
5	5
6	6
7	7
8	8
9	9
10	10
11	11
12	12
13	13
14	14
15	15
16	16
17	17
18	18
19	19
20	20
21	21
22	22
23	23
24	24
25	25
26	26
27	27
28	28
29	29
30	30
31	31
32	32
33	33
34	34
35	35
36	36
37	37
38	38
39	39
40	40

(a)

(b)

Name

Section

Date

1		1
2		2
3		3
4		4
5		5
6		6
7		7
8		8
9		9
10		10
11		11
12		12
13		13
14		14
15		15
16		16
17		17
18		18
19		19
20		20
21		21
22		22
23		23
24		24
25		25
26		26
27		27
28		28
29		29
30		30
31		31
32		32
33		33
34		34
35		35
36		36
37		37
38		38
39		39
40		40

Name

Section

Date

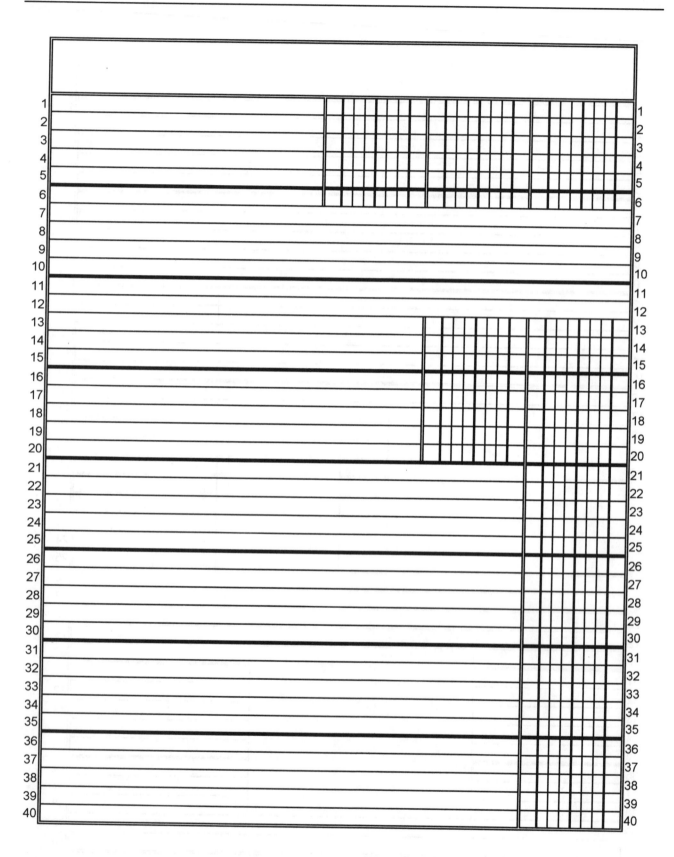

Name

Section

Date

#1　(a)

(b)

#3　(a)

(b)

(c)

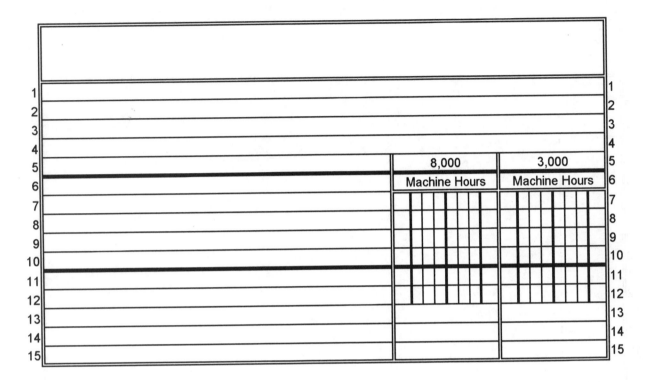

		8,000 Machine Hours	3,000 Machine Hours	
1				1
2				2
3				3
4				4
5				5
6				6
7				7
8				8
9				9
10				10
11				11
12				12
13				13
14				14
15				15

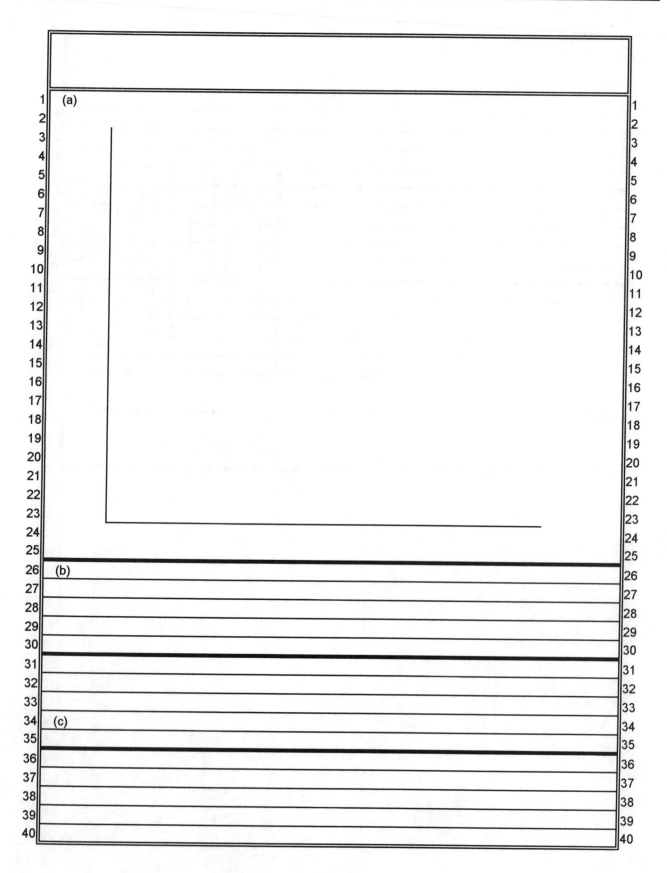

Name

Section

Date

#5   (a)

(b)

#6   (a)

(b)

(c)

#7

	August Results (Base Amounts)	Alternative		
		1 Increase Selling Price by 10%	2 Decrease Variable Costs to 65% of Sales	3 Reduce Fixed Costs by $10,000
Sales				
Less: Variable Costs				
Fixed Costs				
Net Income				

#8

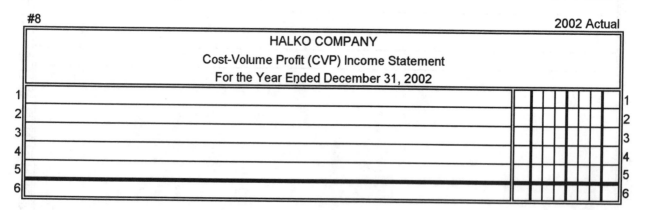

2002 Actual

HALKO COMPANY
Cost-Volume Profit (CVP) Income Statement
For the Year Ended December 31, 2002

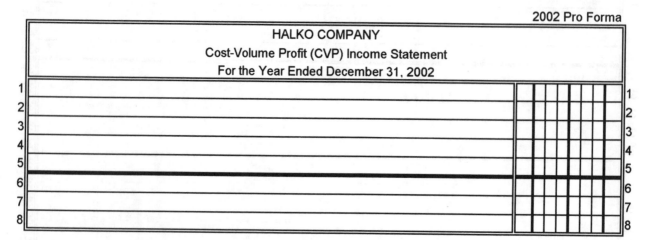

2002 Pro Forma

HALKO COMPANY
Cost-Volume Profit (CVP) Income Statement
For the Year Ended December 31, 2002

(b)

AFN COMPANY Income Statement (Absorption Costing) For the Year Ended December 31,	2002	2003
1		
2		
3		
4		
5		
6		
7		
8		
9		
10		
11		
12		
13		
14		
15		
16		
17		
18		

(c)

	2002	2003
Variable Costing income		
Absorption costing income		

(a)

	Variable cost (per haircut)		Fixed cost (per month)	
1				1
2				2
3				3
4				4
5				5
6				6
7				7
8				8
9				9

(b) (1) Break-even sales in units   **(2) Break-even sales in dollars**

10	10
11	11
12	12
13	13
14	14
15	15

(c) CVP graph

16	16
17	17
18	18
19	19
20	20
21	21
22	22
23	23
24	24
25	25
26	26
27	27
28	28
29	29
30	30
31	31
32	32
33	33
34	34
35	35

(d) Net income

36		36
37		37
38		38
39		39
40		40

(a)

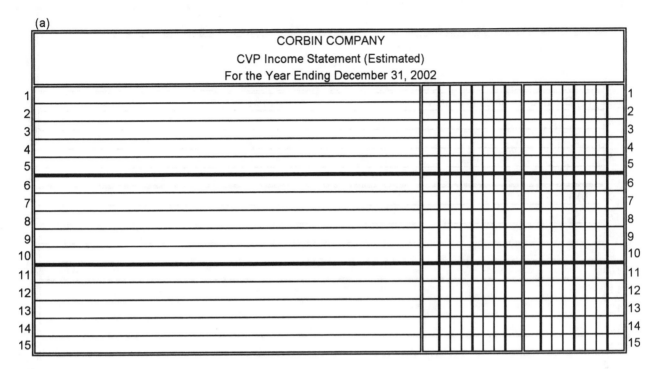

CORBIN COMPANY
CVP Income Statement (Estimated)
For the Year Ending December 31, 2002

(b), (c), and (d)

(b)

(1) Break-even sales in units   (2) Break-even sales in dollars

(c) Contribution margin ratio

Margin of safety ratio

(d) Required sales

(a) Break-even sales in dollars	
(b) 1.	
2.	
3.	
Recommendation	

(a) and (b)

1	(a) Current break-even point:
2	
3	
4	
5	
6	
7	
8	New break-even point:
9	
10	
11	
12	
13	(b) Current margin-of-safety percentage:
14	
15	
16	
17	
18	New margin-of-safety percentage:
19	
20	
21	
22	

(c)

THRIFTY SHOE STORE

Comparative CVP Income Statement

	Current	Proposed
1		
2		
3		
4		
5		
6		
7		
8		
9		
10		
11		
12		
13		

(a)

ZAKI METAL COMPANY Income Statement (Variable Costing) For the Year Ended December 31,	2002	2003
1		
2		
3		
4		
5		
6		
7		
8		
9		
10		
11		
12		
13		
14		
15		
16		
17		
18		
19		
20		
21		
22		
23		
24		
25		

(d)

1	
2	
3	
4	
5	
6	
7	
8	
9	

(b)

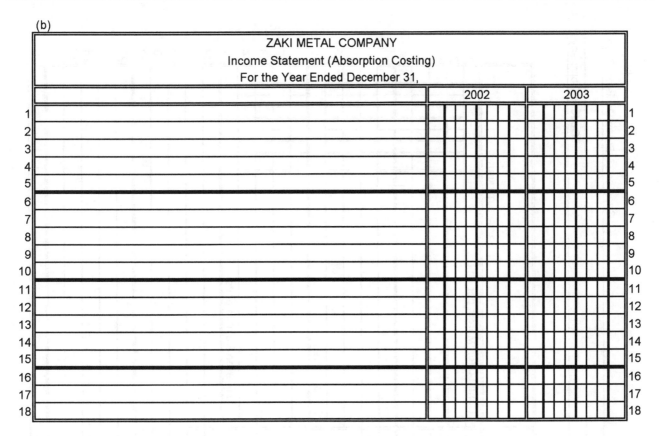

ZAKI METAL COMPANY
Income Statement (Absorption Costing)
For the Year Ended December 31,

	2002	2003
1		
2		
3		
4		
5		
6		
7		
8		
9		
10		
11		
12		
13		
14		
15		
16		
17		
18		

(c)

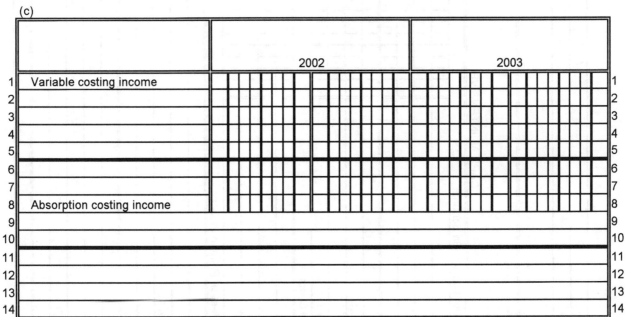

	2002	2003
1 Variable costing income		
2		
3		
4		
5		
6		
7		
8 Absorption costing income		
9		
10		
11		
12		
13		
14		

(a)

CAPITAL INTENSIVE

LABOR INTENSIVE

Contribution Margin per unit:

Contribution Margin per unit:

Fixed Costs

Fixed Costs

Break-even Point in units:

Break-even Point in units:

(b)

(c)

| 1 |
| 2 |
| 3 |
| 4 |
| 5 |
| 6 |
| 7 |
| 8 |
| 9 |
| 10 |
| 11 |
| 12 |
| 13 |
| 14 |
| 15 |
| 16 |
| 17 |
| 18 |
| 19 |
| 20 |
| 21 |
| 22 |
| 23 |
| 24 |
| 25 |
| 26 |
| 27 |

(a) and (b)

1	(a) Variable costs per unit:	
2		
3		
4		
5		
6		
7	Break-even point in dollars:	
8		
9		
10		
11		
12		
13	Break-even point in units:	
14		
15		
16		
17		
18	(b) Computations-	
19		
20		
21		
22		
23		
24	Net income calculation:	
25		
26		
27		
28		
29		
30		
31		
32		
33		
34		
35		
36		
37		
38		
39		
40		

(b) (Continued), (c), and (d)

1	(b) (Continued) - New break-even point in dollars:	
2		
3		
4		
5		
6		
7		
8	(c) Computations-	
9		
10		
11		
12		
13		
14	Net income calculation:	
15		
16		
17		
18		
19		
20		
21		
22		
23		
24		
25		
26		
27		
28		
29		
30		
31	New break-even point in dollars:	
32		
33		
34		
35		
36		
37		
38	(d)	
39		
40		

Name

Section

Date

1	1
2	2
3	3
4	4
5	5
6	6
7	7
8	8
9	9
10	10
11	11
12	12
13	13
14	14
15	15
16	16
17	17
18	18
19	19
20	20
21	21
22	22
23	23
24	24
25	25
26	26
27	27
28	28
29	29
30	30
31	31
32	32
33	33
34	34
35	35

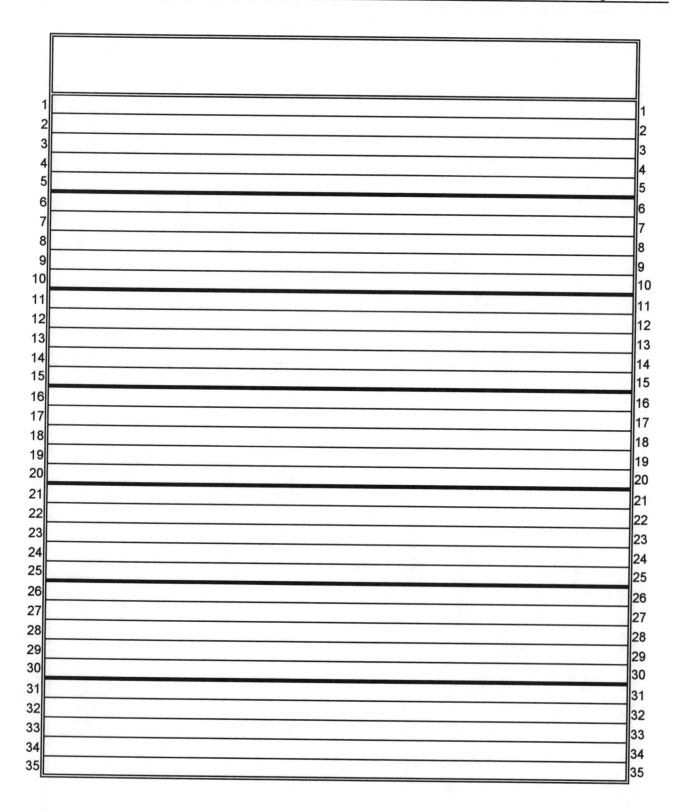

1	(a)
2	
3	
4	
5	
6	
7	(b)
8	
9	
10	
11	
12	
13	
14	
15	(c)
16	
17	
18	
19	
20	

Name

Section

Date

	1
1	
2	2
3	3
4	4
5	5
6	6
7	7
8	8
9	9
10	10
11	11
12	12
13	13
14	14
15	15
16	16
17	17
18	18
19	19
20	20
21	21
22	22
23	23
24	24
25	25
26	26
27	27
28	28
29	29
30	30
31	31
32	32
33	33
34	34
35	35
36	36
37	37
38	38
39	39
40	40

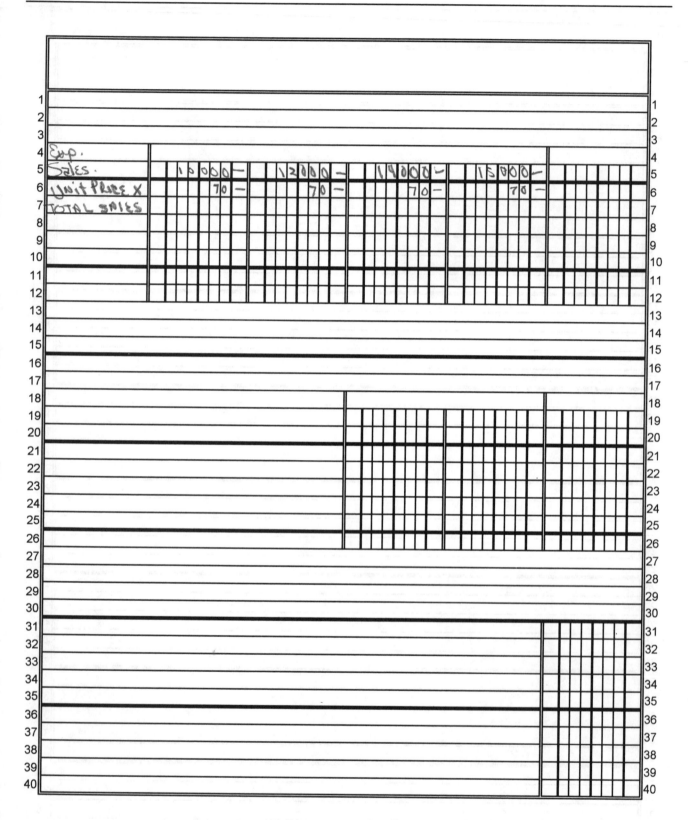

Exp.

Sales.

Unit Price X   70   70   70   70

Total Sales

Name

Section

Date

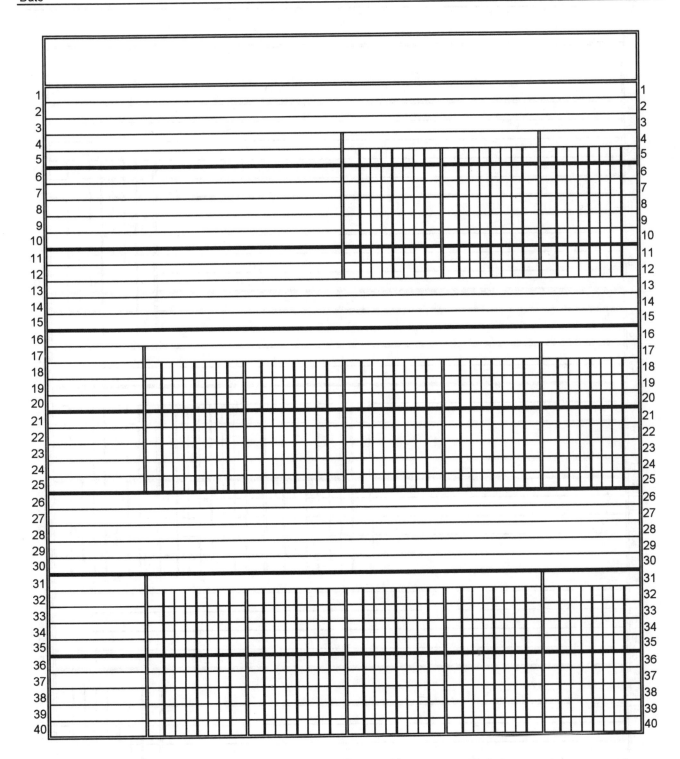

	1		1
2		2
3		3
4		4
5		5
6		6
7		7
8		8
9		9
10		10
11		11
12		12
13		13
14		14
15		15
16		16
17		17
18		18
19		19
20		20
21		21
22		22
23		23
24		24
25		25
26		26
27		27
28		28
29		29
30		30
31		31
32		32
33		33
34		34
35		35
36		36
37		37
38		38
39		39
40		40

L. QUICK ELECTRONICS, INC.
Sales Budget
For the Six Months Ending June 30, 2002

Product	Quarter 1			Quarter 2			Six Months		
	Units	Selling Price	Total Sales	Units	Selling Price	Total Sales	Units	Selling Price	Total Sales
1									
2									
3									
4									
5									
6									
7									
8									
9									
10									
11									
12									
13									
14									
15									

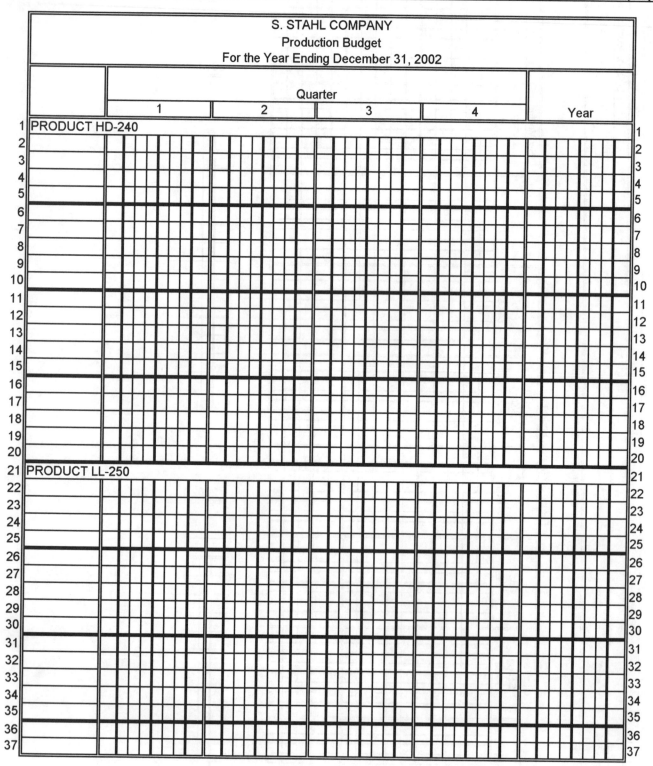

S. STAHL COMPANY
Production Budget
For the Year Ending December 31, 2002

	Quarter				Year
	1	2	3	4	

PRODUCT HD-240

PRODUCT LL-250

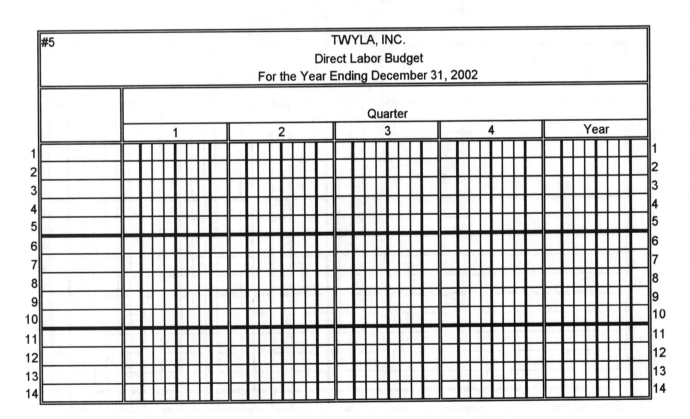

#3

GOSH-BY-GOLLY INDUSTRIES
Direct Materials Budget
For the Quarter Ending March 31, 2003

	January	February	March
1			
2			
3			
4			
5			
6			
7			
8			
9			
10			
11			
12			
13			
14			
15			

#5

TWYLA, INC.
Direct Labor Budget
For the Year Ending December 31, 2002

	Quarter				
	1	2	3	4	Year
1					
2					
3					
4					
5					
6					
7					
8					
9					
10					
11					
12					
13					
14					

(a)

W. SUBLETTE COMPANY
Production Budget
For the Six Months Ended June 30, 2003

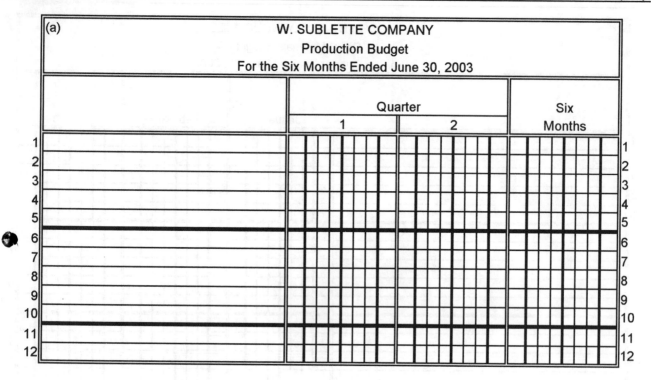

(b)

W. SUBLETTE COMPANY
Direct Materials Budget
For the Six Months Ending June 30, 2003

		Quarter				Year
		1	2	3	4	
1						
2	Variable Costs					
3	Indirect					
4	materials					
5	Indirect					
6	labor					
7	Maintenance					
8						
9	TOTAL					
10						
11	Fixed Costs					
12	Supervisory					
13	salaries					
14	Depreciation					
15						
16	Maintenance					
17						
18	TOTAL					
19						
20	Total Manufact-					
21	uring Overhead					
22						
23						
24	Direct labor					
25	hours					
26						
27	Overhead rate per					
28	direct labor hour					
29						
30						

VINCENT NATHAN COMPANY
Manufacturing Overhead Budget
For the Year Ending December 31, 2002

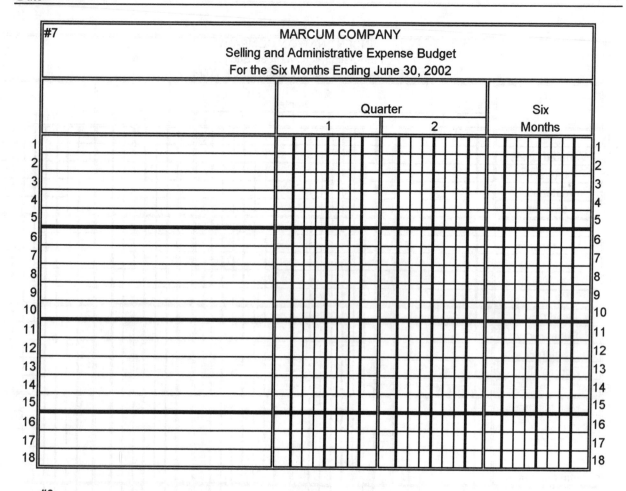

#7

MARCUM COMPANY

Selling and Administrative Expense Budget

For the Six Months Ending June 30, 2002

	Quarter		Six Months
	1	2	

#8

LONGHEAD COMPANY

Budgeted Income Statement

For the Year Ending December 31, 2002

Computation of Cost of Goods Sold

CAMPAGNA COMPANY Cash Budget For the Two Months Ending February 28, 2002	January					Februrary				
1										
2 Beginning Cash Balance	$	4	6	0	0	0	$	3	1	0	0	0
3										
4										
5										
6										
7										
8										
9										
10										
11										
12										
13										
14										
15										
16										
17										
18										
19										
20										
21										
22										
23										
24										
25										
26										
27										
28										
29										
30										

(a)

SHERRICK STORES

Merchandise Purchases Budget

For the Month Ending June 30, 2002

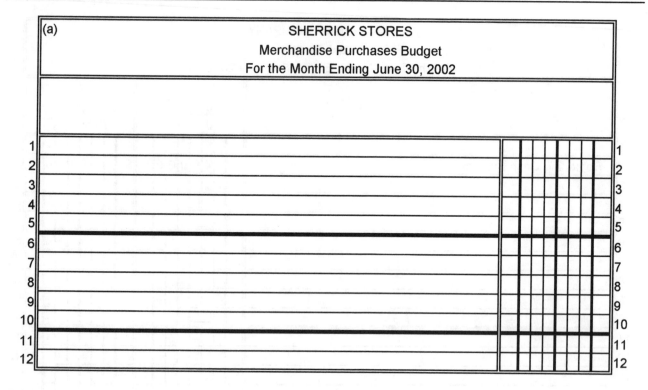

(b)

SHERRICK STORES

Budgeted Income Statement

For the Month Ending June 30, 2002

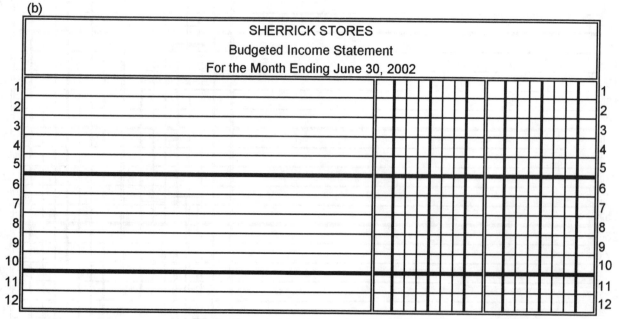

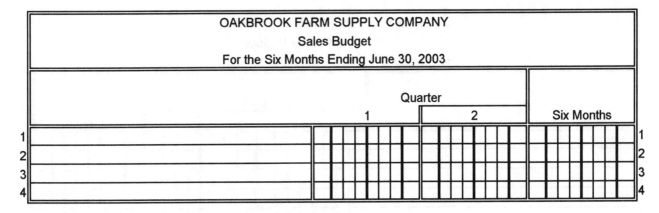

OAKBROOK FARM SUPPLY COMPANY

Sales Budget

For the Six Months Ending June 30, 2003

	Quarter		Six Months
	1	2	
1			
2			
3			
4			

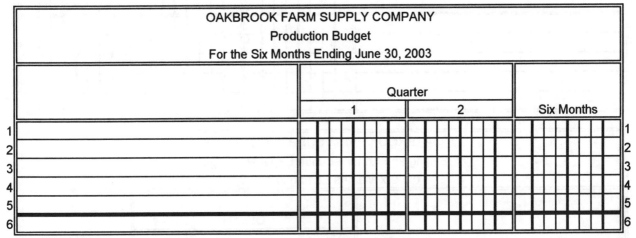

OAKBROOK FARM SUPPLY COMPANY

Production Budget

For the Six Months Ending June 30, 2003

	Quarter		Six Months
	1	2	
1			
2			
3			
4			
5			
6			

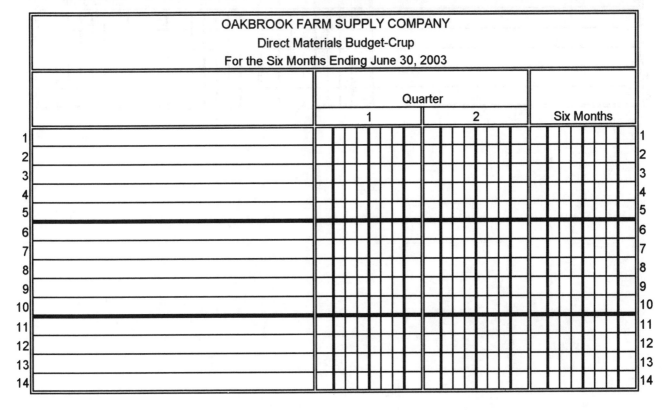

OAKBROOK FARM SUPPLY COMPANY

Direct Materials Budget-Crup

For the Six Months Ending June 30, 2003

	Quarter		Six Months
	1	2	
1			
2			
3			
4			
5			
6			
7			
8			
9			
10			
11			
12			
13			
14			

OAKBROOK FARM SUPPLY COMPANY

Direct Labor Budget

For the Six Months Ending June 30, 2003

	Quarter		Six Months
	1	2	
1			
2			
3			
4			
5			
6			
7			
8			
9			
10			

OAKBROOK FARM SUPPLY COMPANY

Selling and Administrative Expense Budget

For the Six Months Ending June 30, 2003

	Quarter		Six Months
	1	2	
1			
2			
3			
4			
5			

Section

Date

(a)

	January	February
(1) Expected collections from customers		
(2) Expected payments for direct materials		

(b)

YAEGER COMPANY
Cash Budget
For the Two Months Ending February 28, 2003

	January	February
Beginning cash balance		

(a)

HENNING COMPANY-San Miguel Store
Merchandise Purchases Budget
For the Months of July and August, 2003

	May	June
1		
2		
3		
4		
5		
6		
7		
8		

(b)

HENNING COMPANY-San Miguel Store
Budgeted Income Statement
For the Months of July and August, 2003

	May	June
1		
2		
3		
4		
5		
6		
7		
8		
9		
10		
11		
12		
13		
14		
15		
16		
17		
18		
19		
20		
21		
22		
23		
24		

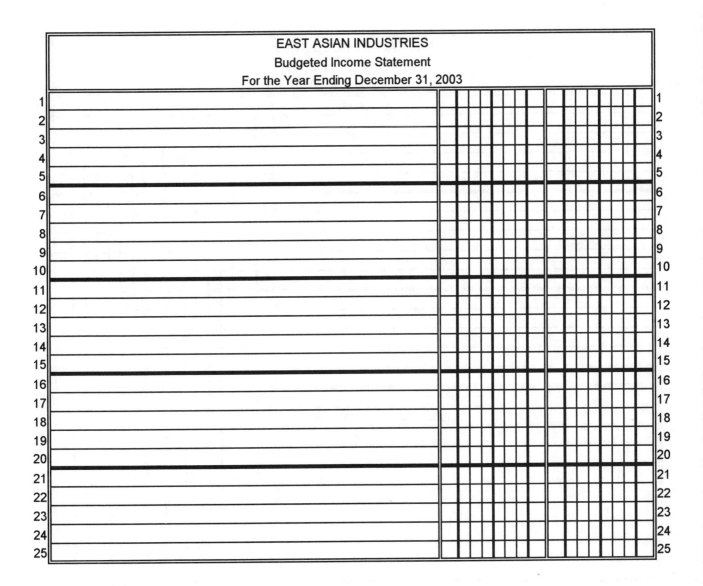

EAST ASIAN INDUSTRIES

Budgeted Income Statement

For the Year Ending December 31, 2003

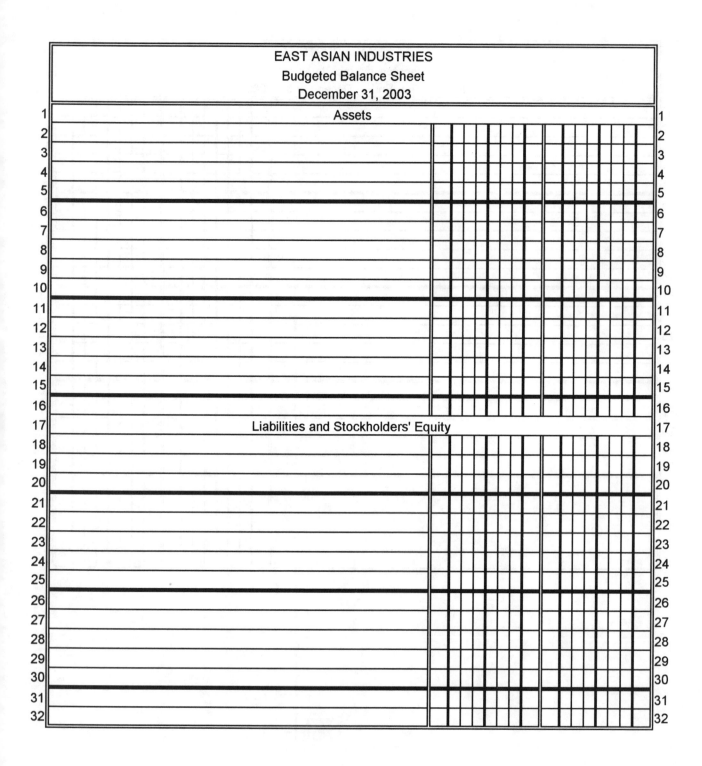

EAST ASIAN INDUSTRIES
Budgeted Balance Sheet
December 31, 2003

Assets

Liabilities and Stockholders' Equity

ALCORN FARM SUPPLY COMPANY

Sales Budget

For the Six Months Ending June 30, 2002

	Quarter		Six Months
	1	2	
1			
2			
3			
4			

ALCORN FARM SUPPLY COMPANY

Production Budget

For the Six Months Ending June 30, 2002

	Quarter		Six Months
	1	2	
1			
2			
3			
4			
5			
6			

ALCORN FARM SUPPLY COMPANY

Direct Materials Budget-Crup

For the Six Months Ending June 30, 2002

	Quarter		Six Months
	1	2	
1			
2			
3			
4			
5			
6			
7			
8			
9			
10			
11			
12			
13			
14			

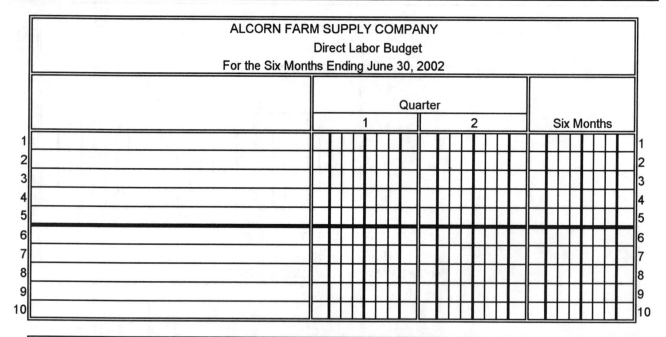

ALCORN FARM SUPPLY COMPANY
Direct Labor Budget
For the Six Months Ending June 30, 2002

	Quarter		Six Months
	1	2	
1			
2			
3			
4			
5			
6			
7			
8			
9			
10			

ALCORN FARM SUPPLY COMPANY
Selling and Administrative Expense Budget
For the Six Months Ending June 30, 2002

	Quarter		Six Months
	1	2	
1			
2			
3			
4			
5			

ALCORN FARM SUPPLY COMPANY	
Budgeted Income Statement	
For the Six Months Ending June 30, 2002	

ALCORN FARM SUPPLY COMPANY			
Schedule-Standard Cost Per Bag			
Cost Element	Quantity	Unit Cost	Total

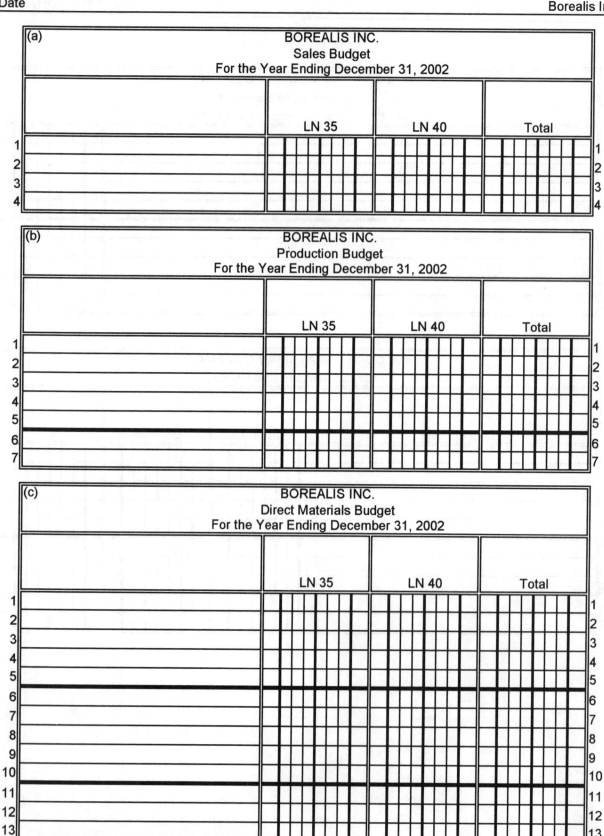

(a)

BOREALIS INC.
Sales Budget
For the Year Ending December 31, 2002

	LN 35	LN 40	Total
1			
2			
3			
4			

(b)

BOREALIS INC.
Production Budget
For the Year Ending December 31, 2002

	LN 35	LN 40	Total
1			
2			
3			
4			
5			
6			
7			

(c)

BOREALIS INC.
Direct Materials Budget
For the Year Ending December 31, 2002

	LN 35	LN 40	Total
1			
2			
3			
4			
5			
6			
7			
8			
9			
10			
11			
12			
13			

(d)

BOREALIS INC.
Direct Labor Budget
For the Year Ending December 31, 2002

	LN 35	LN 40	Total
1			
2			
3			
4			
5			
6			
7			
8			
9			
10			

(e)

BOREALIS INC.
Budgeted Income Statement
For the Year Ending December 31, 2002

	LN 35	LN 40	Total
1			
2			
3			
4			
5			
6			
7			
8			
9			
10			
11			
12			
13			
14			
15			
16			
17			
18			
19			
20			

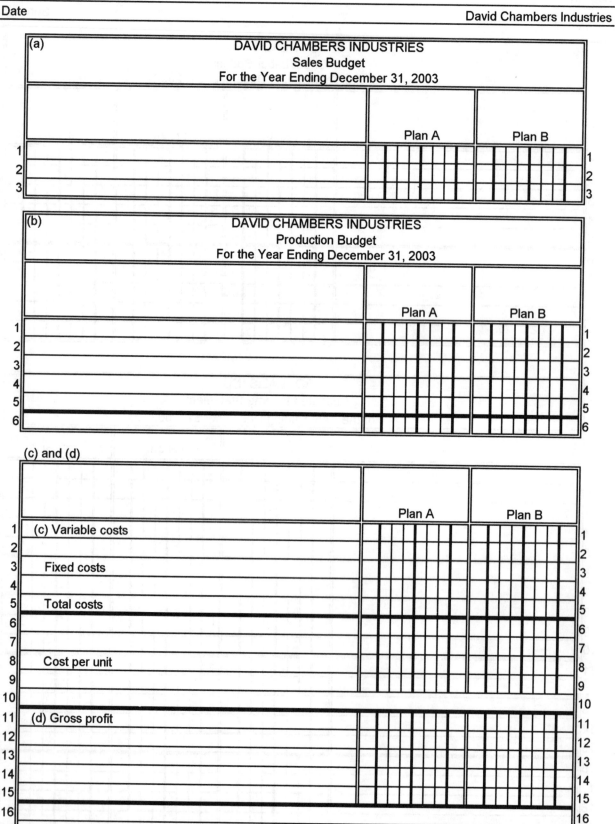

(a)

DAVID CHAMBERS INDUSTRIES
Sales Budget
For the Year Ending December 31, 2003

	Plan A	Plan B
1		
2		
3		

(b)

DAVID CHAMBERS INDUSTRIES
Production Budget
For the Year Ending December 31, 2003

	Plan A	Plan B
1		
2		
3		
4		
5		
6		

(c) and (d)

	Plan A	Plan B
1	(c) Variable costs		
2			
3	Fixed costs		
4			
5	Total costs		
6			
7			
8	Cost per unit		
9			
10			
11	(d) Gross profit		
12			
13			
14			
15			
16			
17			

(a)

	January	February
1. (1) Expected collections from customers		
2.		
3.		
4.		
5.		
6.		
7. (2) Expected payments for direct materials		
8.		
9.		
10.		
11.		
12.		

(b)

FLYPAPER COMPANY
Cash Budget
For the Two Months Ending February 28, 2003

	January	February
1. Beginning cash balance		
2.		
3.		
4.		
5.		
6.		
7.		
8.		
9.		
10.		
11.		
12.		
13.		
14.		
15.		
16.		
17.		
18.		
19.		
20.		
21.		

(a)

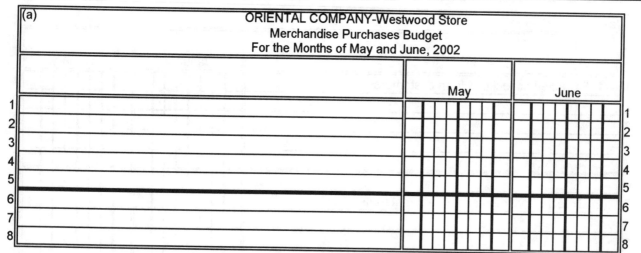

	May	June
1		
2		
3		
4		
5		
6		
7		
8		

(b)

ORIENTAL COMPANY-Westwood Store

Budgeted Income Statement

For the Months of May and June, 2002

	May	June
1		
2		
3		
4		
5		
6		
7		
8		
9		
10		
11		
12		
13		
14		
15		
16		
17		
18		
19		
20		
21		
22		
23		
24		

(a)

	1
1	
2	2
3	3
4	4
5	5
6	6
7	7
8	8
9	9
10	10
11	11
12	12
13	13
14	14
15	15
16	16
17	17
18	18
19	19
20	20
21	21
22	22
23	23
24	24
25	25
26	26
27	27
28	28
29	29
30	30
31	31
32	32
33	33
34	34
35	35
36	36
37	37
38	38
39	39
40	40

(b) and (c)

(b)

(c)

(a)

(b)

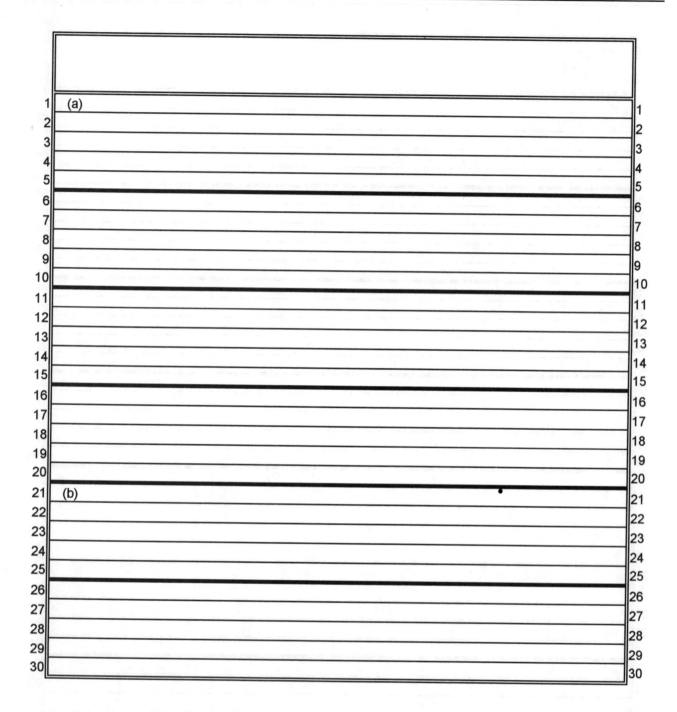

(a)

(b)

Name

Section

Date

1	1
2	2
3	3
4	4
5	5
6	6
7	7
8	8
9	9
10	10
11	11
12	12
13	13
14	14
15	15
16	16
17	17
18	18
19	19
20	20
21	21
22	22
23	23
24	24
25	25
26	26
27	27
28	28
29	29
30	30
31	31
32	32
33	33
34	34
35	35
36	36
37	37
38	38
39	39
40	40

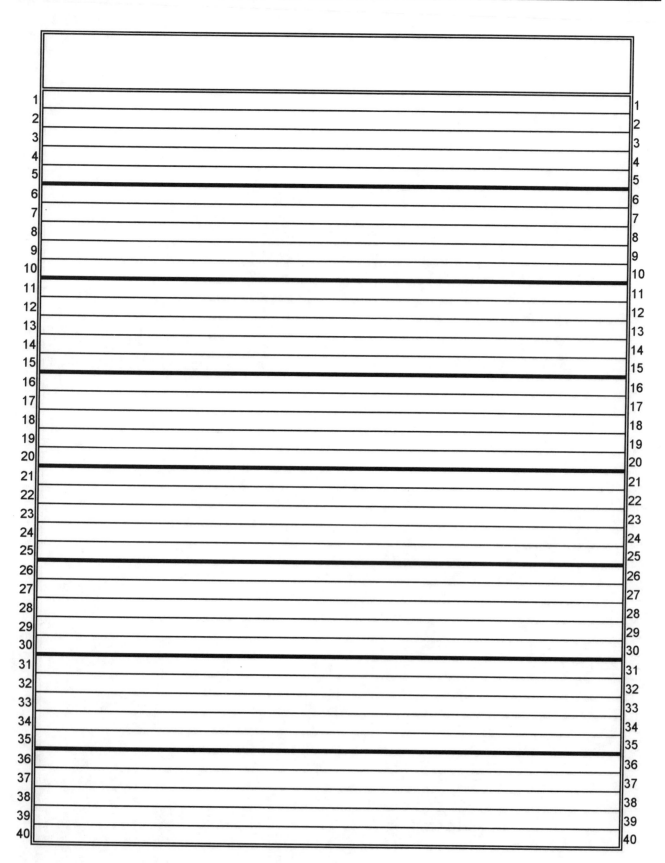

Name

Section

Date

1	1
2	2
3	3
4	4
5	5
6	6
7	7
8	8
9	9
10	10
11	11
12	12
13	13
14	14
15	15
16	16
17	17
18	18
19	19
20	20
21	21
22	22
23	23
24	24
25	25
26	26
27	27
28	28
29	29
30	30
31	31
32	32
33	33
34	34
35	35
36	36
37	37
38	38
39	39
40	40

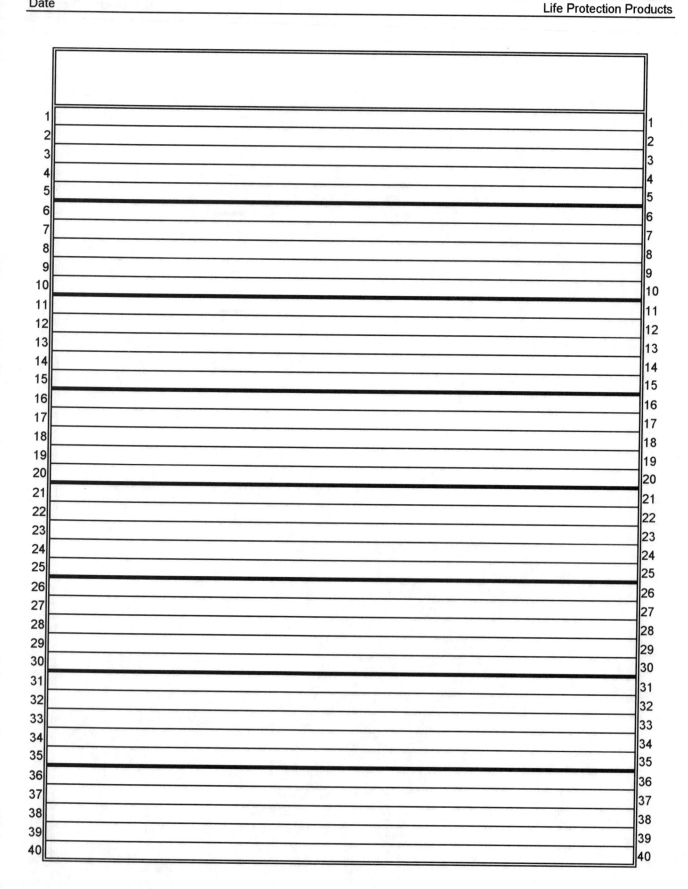

1 (a)	1
2	2
3	3
4	4
5	5
6 (b)	6
7	7
8	8
9	9
10	10
11 (c)	11
12	12
13	13
14	14
15	15
16	16
17	17
18	18
19	19
20	20

Name

Section

Date

	Budget	Actual	Difference
1			
2			
3			
4			
5			
6			
7			
8			
9			
10			
11			
12			
13			
14			
15			
16			
17			
18			
19			
20			
21			
22			
23			
24			
25			
26			
27			
28			
29			
30			
31			
32			
33			
34			
35			
36			
37			
38			
39			
40			

	Budget	Actual	Difference
1			
2			
3			
4			
5			
6			
7			
8			
9			
10			
11			
12			
13			
14			
15			
16			
17			
18			
19			
20			
21			
22			
23			
24			
25			
26			
27			
28			
29			
30			
31			
32			
33			
34			
35			
36			
37			
38			
39			
40			

Name

Section

Date

	Budget	Actual	Difference
1			
2			
3			
4			
5			
6			
7			
8			
9			
10			
11			
12			
13			
14			
15			
16			
17			
18			
19			
20			
21			
22			
23			
24			
25			
26			
27			
28			
29			
30			
31			
32			
33			
34			
35			
36			
37			
38			
39			
40			

1	**# 1**				
2	Activity level				
3	Direct labor hours	7 0 0 0 00	8 0 0 0 00	9 0 0 0 00	1 0 0 0 0 00
4					
5					
6					
7					
8					
9					
10					
11					
12					
13					
14					
15					
16					
17					
18					
19					
20					
21					
22	**# 2**(c)				
23					
24					
25					
26					
27					
28					
29					
30					
31					
32					
33					
34					
35					
36					
37					
38					
39					
40					

	Budget at	Actual Costs	Difference Favorable F Unfavorable U
(a)			
(b)			

Name | Exercises 25-3 and 25-4 (c)

Section

Date | Samano Company

# 3				
Activity level				
Sales	$ 170000	$ 180000	$ 190000	$ 200000

 # 4 (c)

	Budget at	Actual Costs	Difference Favorable F Unfavorable U
1 (a)			
2			
3			
4			
5			
6			
7			
8			
9			
10			
11			
12			
13			
14			
15			
16			
17			
18			
19			
20			
21 (b)			
22			
23			
24			
25			
26			
27			
28			
29			
30			
31			
32			
33			
34			
35			
36			
37			
38			
39			
40			

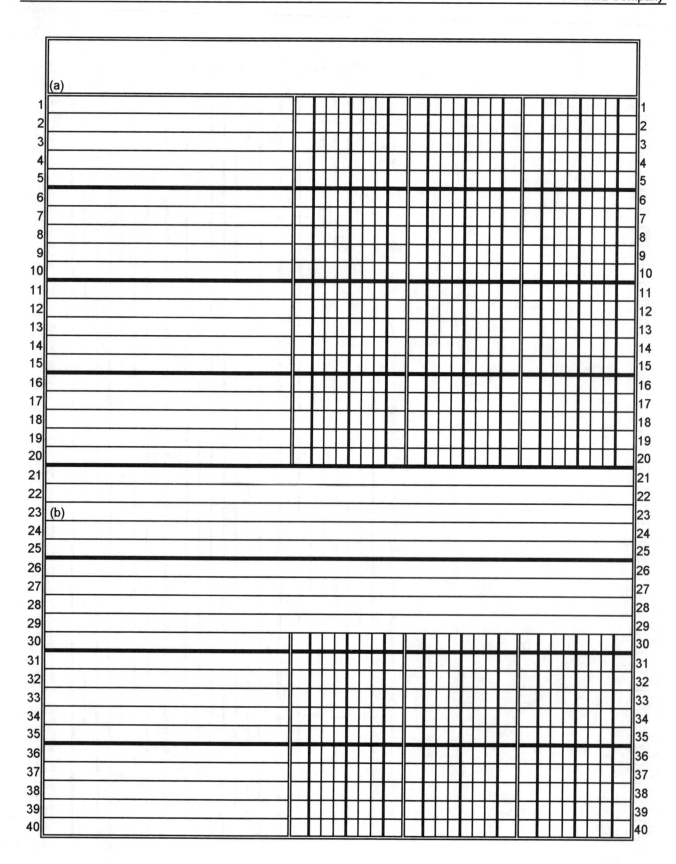

(a)	Budget	Actual	Difference Favorable F Unfavorable U
1			
2			
3			
4			
5			
6			
7			
8			
9			
10			
11			
12			
13			
14			
15			
16			
17			
18			
19			
20			
21			
22			
23			
24			
25			

(b)

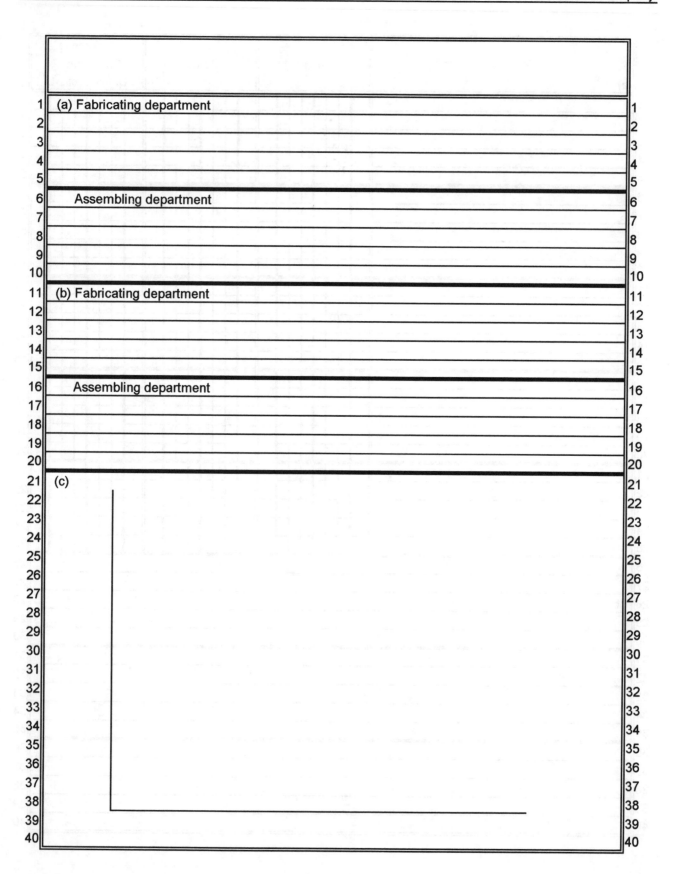

1	(a) Fabricating department
2	
3	
4	
5	
6	Assembling department
7	
8	
9	
10	
11	(b) Fabricating department
12	
13	
14	
15	
16	Assembling department
17	
18	
19	
20	
21	(c)
22	
23	
24	
25	
26	
27	
28	
29	
30	
31	
32	
33	
34	
35	
36	
37	
38	
39	
40	

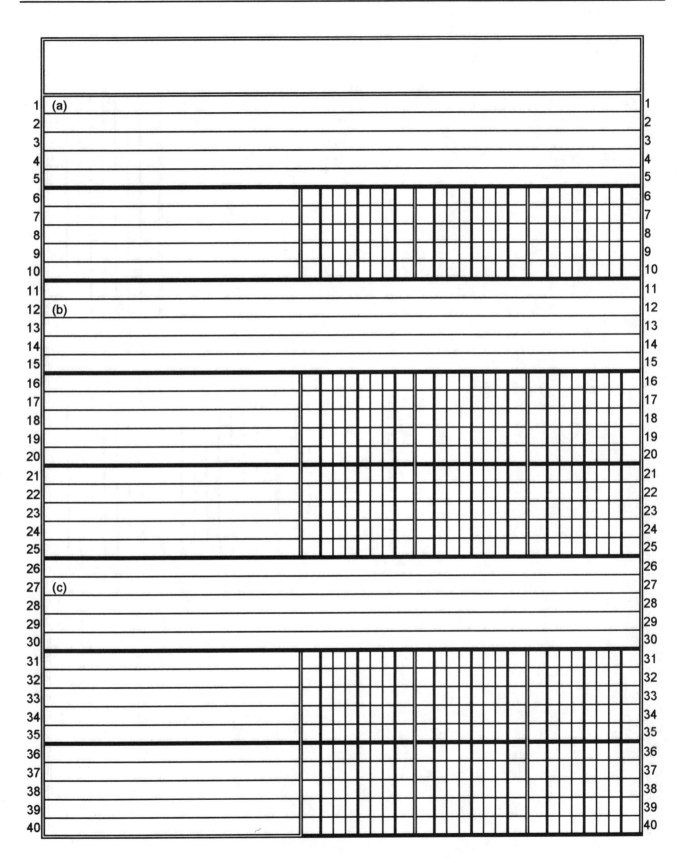

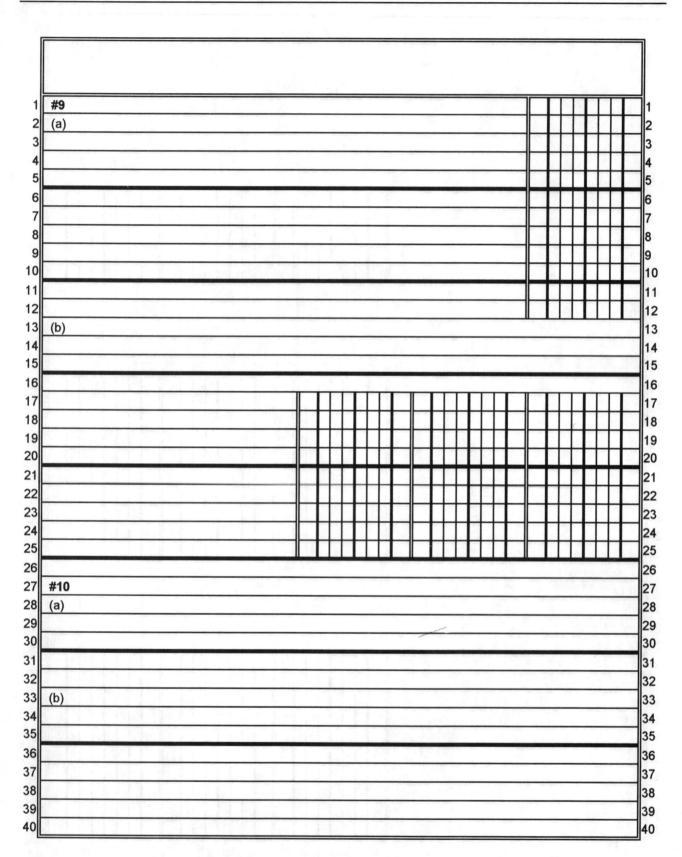

#9

(a)

(b)

#10

(a)

(b)

(a)

WAHLEN COMPANY
Monthly Flexible Manufacturing Overhead Budget
Ironing Department
For the Year 2002

Activity level Direct labor hours	3 5 0 0 0	4 0 0 0 0	4 5 0 0 0	5 0 0 0 0
1				
2				
3				
4				
5				
6				
7				
8				
9				
10				
11				
12				
13				
14				

(b)

WAHLEN COMPANY
Ironing Department
Manufacturing Overhead Budget Report (Flexible)
For the Month Ended June 30, 2002

Direct labor hours Expected = Actual =	Budgeted at	Actual Costs	Difference Favorable F Unfavorable U
1			
2			
3			
4			
5			
6			
7			
8			
9			
10			
11			
12			
13			
14			

(c) and (d)

(e)

(a)

1	1
2	2
3	3

(b)

NIGH COMPANY
Assembling Department
Budget Report (Flexible)
For the Month Ended August 31, 2002

Units Expected = Actual =	Budgeted at	Actual Costs	Difference Favorable F Unfavorable U
1			
2			
3			
4			
5			
6			
7			
8			
9			
10			
11			
12			
13			
14			
15			
16			
17			
18			
19			
20			
21			
22			
23			
24			
25			

(c)

NIGH COMPANY							
Assembling Department							
Budget Report (Flexible)							
For the Month Ended September 30, 2002							
Units Expected = Actual =			Budgeted at	Actual Costs	Difference Favorable F Unfavorable U		
1							
2							
3							
4							
5							
6							
7							
8							
9							
10							
11							
12							
13							
14							
15							
16							
17							
18							
19							
20							
21							
22							
23							
24							
25							

(a)

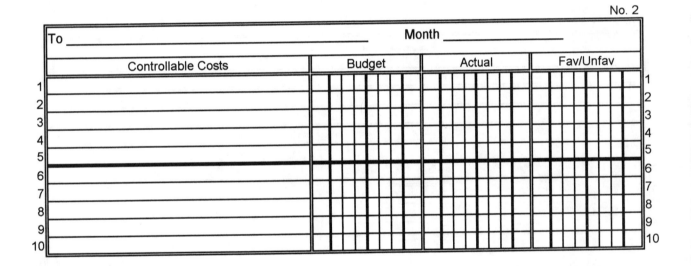

Name _____
Section _____
Date _____

Problem 25-6A Concluded

Tilg Company

(a) Continu

No. 4

| To _____ | Month _____ |
Controllable Costs	Budget	Actual	Fav/Unfav

(b)

1.

2.

3.

(a)

GREISH COMPANY

Assembly Department

Monthly Flexible Manufacturing Overhead Budget

For the Year 2002

Activity level Direct labor hours	18 000	20 000	22 000	24 000
1				
2				
3				
4				
5				
6				
7				
8				
9				
10				
11				
12				
13				
14				
15				
16				
17				
18				

(b)

GREISH COMPANY
Assembly Department
Manufacturing Overhead Budget Report (Flexible)
For the Month Ended January 31, 2002

Direct labor hours Expected = Actual =	Budgeted at	Actual Costs	Difference Favorable F Unfavorable U
1			
2			
3			
4			
5			
6			
7			
8			
9			
10			
11			
12			
13			
14			
15			
16			
17			

(c)

1	
2	
3	
4	
5	

(a)

JUDS MANUFACTURING COMPANY
Monthly Flexible Manufacturing Overhead Budget
Assembly Department
For the Year 2002

Activity level Direct labor hours	2 2 5 0 0	2 5 0 0 0	2 7 5 0 0	3 0 0 0 0
1				
2				
3				
4				
5				
6				
7				
8				
9				
10				
11				
12				
13				
14				

(b)

JUDS MANUFACTURING COMPANY
Assembly Department
Manufacturing Overhead Budget Report (Flexible)
For the Month Ended July 31, 2002

Direct labor hours Expected = Actual =	Budgeted at	Actual Costs	Difference Favorable F Unfavorable U
1			
2			
3			
4			
5			
6			
7			
8			
9			
10			
11			
12			
13			
14			

(c) and (d)

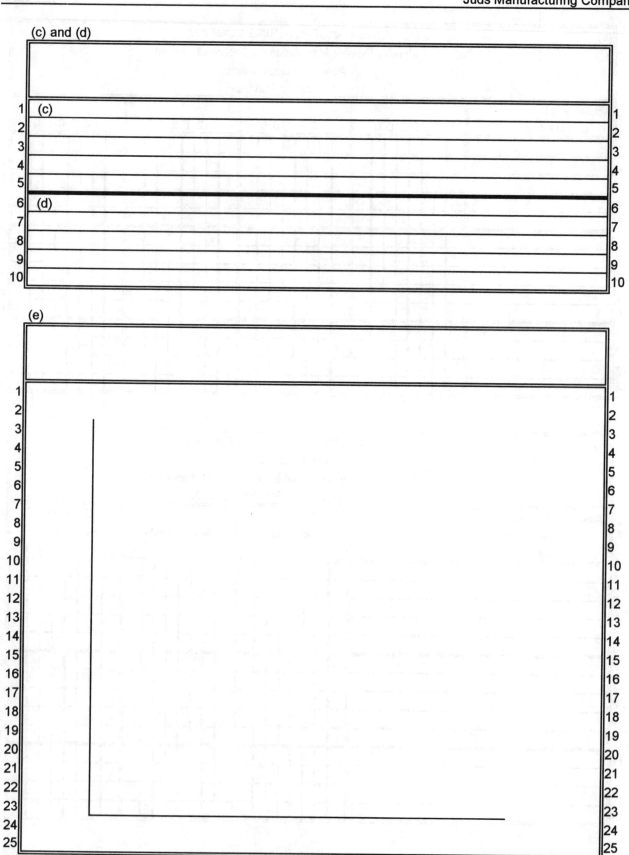

(c)

1
2
3
4
5
6
7
8
9
10

(d)

(e)

1
2
3
4
5
6
7
8
9
10
11
12
13
14
15
16
17
18
19
20
21
22
23
24
25

	(a)		1
1			2
2			3
3			

(b)

LORCH COMPANY

Packaging Department

Budget Report (Flexible)

For the Month Ended May 31, 2002

Units Expected = Actual =	Budgeted at	Actual Costs	Difference Favorable F Unfavorable U	
1				1
2				2
3				3
4				4
5				5
6				6
7				7
8				8
9				9
10				10
11				11
12				12
13				13
14				14
15				15
16				16
17				17
18				18
19				19
20				20
21				21
22				22
23				23
24				24
25				25

(c)

LORCH COMPANY			
Packaging Department			
Budget Report (Flexible)			
For the Month Ended June 30, 2002			
Units Expected = Actual =	Budgeted at	Actual Costs	Difference Favorable F Unfavorable U

(a)

PETERS MANUFACTURING INC
Home Appliance Division
Management Responsibility Report
For the Year Ended December 31, 2002

	Budget	Actual	Difference Favorable F Unfavorable U
1			
2			
3			
4			
5			
6			
7			
8			
9			
10			
11			
12			
13			
14			
15			

(b)

1	
2	
3	
4	
5	
6	
7	
8	
9	
10	
11	
12	
13	
14	
15	
16 **(c)**	
17	
18	

(a)

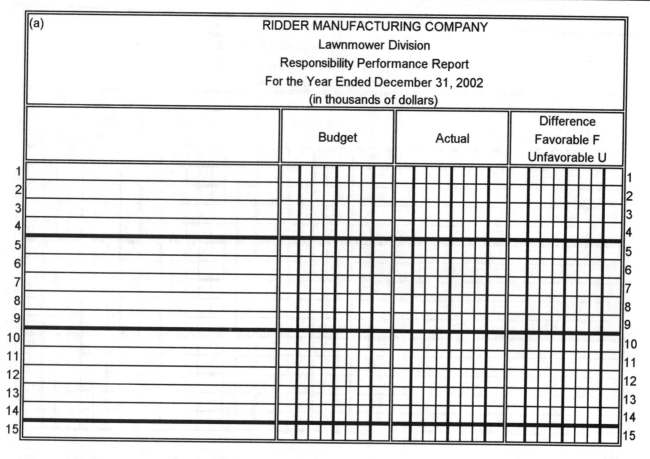

RIDDER MANUFACTURING COMPANY
Lawnmower Division
Responsibility Performance Report
For the Year Ended December 31, 2002
(in thousands of dollars)

	Budget	Actual	Difference Favorable F Unfavorable U
1			
2			
3			
4			
5			
6			
7			
8			
9			
10			
11			
12			
13			
14			
15			

(b)

(c) 1.

2.

3.

(b) Continued

1	1
2	2
3	3
4	4
5	5
6	6
7	7
8	8
9	9
10	10
11	11
12	12
13	13
14	14
15	15
16	16
17	17
18	18
19	19
20	20
21	21
22	22
23	23
24	24
25	25
26	26
27	27
28	28
29	29
30	30
31	31
32	32
33	33
34	34
35	35
36	36
37	37
38	38
39	39
40	40

(a)

(b)

		1
1 Number of Guests		1
2		2
3 Variable Costs:		3
4		4
5		5
6		6
7		7
8		8
9		9
10		10
11		11
12 Fixed Costs:		12
13		13
14		14
15		15
16		16
17		17
18		18
19		19
20		20
21		21
22		22
23		23
24		24
25		25
26		26
27		27
28		28
29		29
30		30
31		31
32		32
33		33
34		34
35		35
36		36
37		37
38		38
39		39
40		40

(a) and (b)

1	(a)
2	
3	
4	
5	
6	(b)
7	
8	
9	
10	
11	

(c)

REEBLES COMPANY
Production Department
Manufacturing Overhead Budget Report (Flexible)
For the Month Ended

Units Expected = Actual =	Budgeted at	Actual at	Difference Favorable F Unfavorable U
1			
2			
3			
4			
5			
6			
7			
8			
9			
10			
11			
12			
13			
14			
15			
16			
17			
18			
19			
20			
21			

(d)

	Budget	Actual	Difference Favorable F Unfavorable U
REEBLES COMPANY			
Production Department			
Manufacturing Overhead Responsibility Report			
For The Month Ended			
Controllable Cost			

(a)

(b)

(c)

1	1
2	2
3	3
4	4
5	5
6	6
7	7
8	8
9	9
10	10
11	11
12	12
13	13
14	14
15	15
16	16
17	17
18	18
19	19
20	20
21	21
22	22
23	23
24	24
25	25
26	26
27	27
28	28
29	29
30	30
31	31
32	32
33	33
34	34
35	35
36	36
37	37
38	38
39	39
40	40

	1		1
2		2	
3		3	
4		4	
5		5	
6		6	
7		7	
8		8	
9		9	
10		10	
11		11	
12		12	
13		13	
14		14	
15		15	
16		16	
17		17	
18		18	
19		19	
20		20	
21		21	
22		22	
23		23	
24		24	
25		25	
26		26	
27		27	
28		28	
29		29	
30		30	
31		31	
32		32	
33		33	
34		34	
35		35	
36		36	
37		37	
38		38	
39		39	
40		40	

1			1
2			2
3			3
4			4
5			5
6			6
7			7
8			8
9			9
10			10
11			11
12			12
13			13
14			14
15			15
16			16
17			17
18			18
19			19
20			20
21			21
22			22
23			23
24			24
25			25
26			26
27			27
28			28
29			29
30			30
31			31
32			32
33			33
34			34
35			35
36			36
37			37
38			38
39			39
40			40

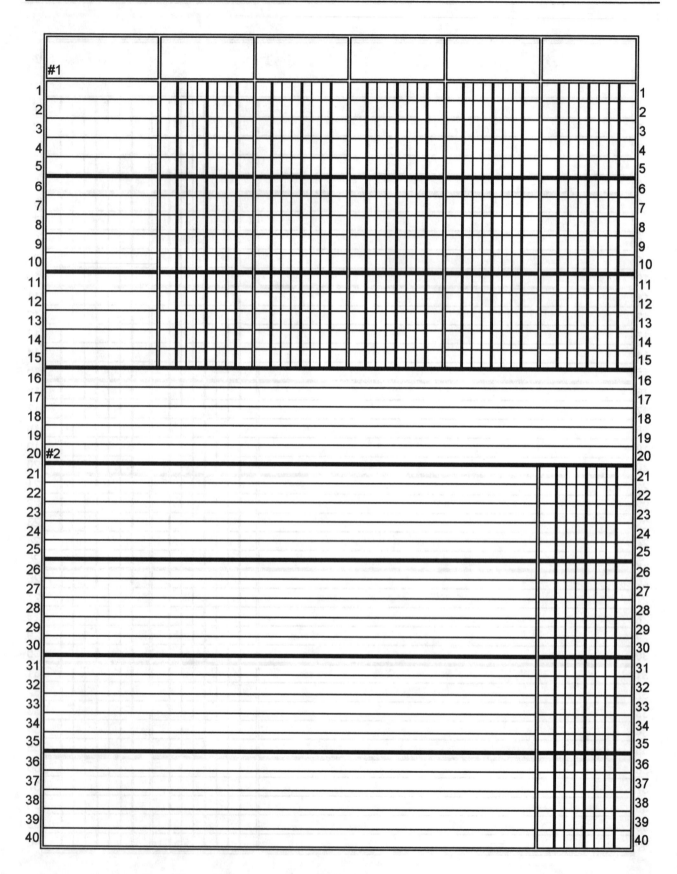

#3

1		1
2		2
3		3
4		4
5		5
6		6
7		7
8		8
9		9
10		10
11		11
12		12
13		13
14		14
15		15
16		16
17		17
18		18
19		19
20		20

#4

21		21
22		22
23		23
24		24
25		25
26		26
27		27
28		28
29		29
30		30
31		31
32		32
33		33
34		34
35		35
36		36
37		37
38		38
39		39
40		40

Materials Variance Matrix (not required)

Labor Variance Matrix (not required)

#5

#7

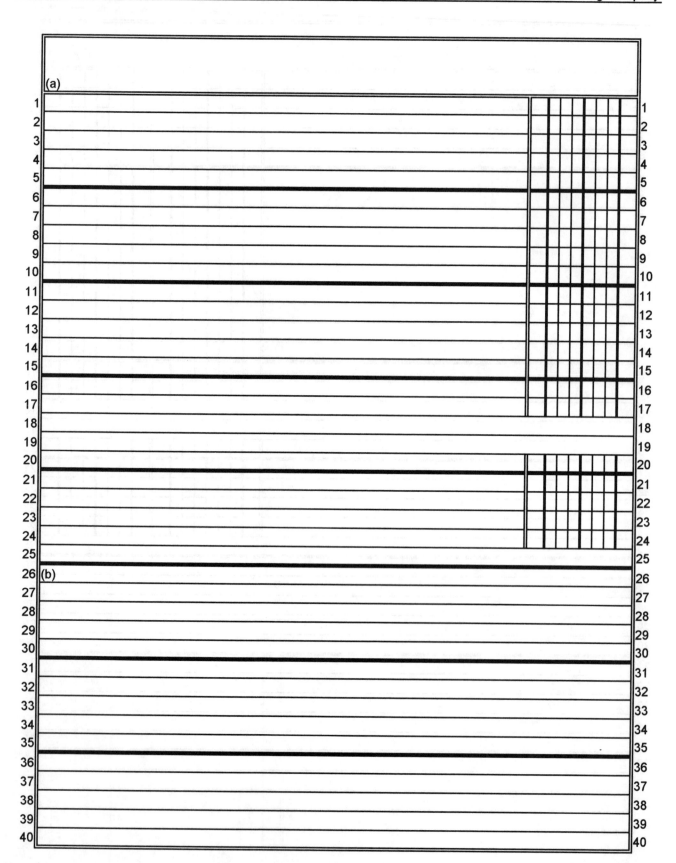

(a)

(b)

(a)

Manufacturing Overhead Variance Matrix (not required)

(b)

(b)

#9

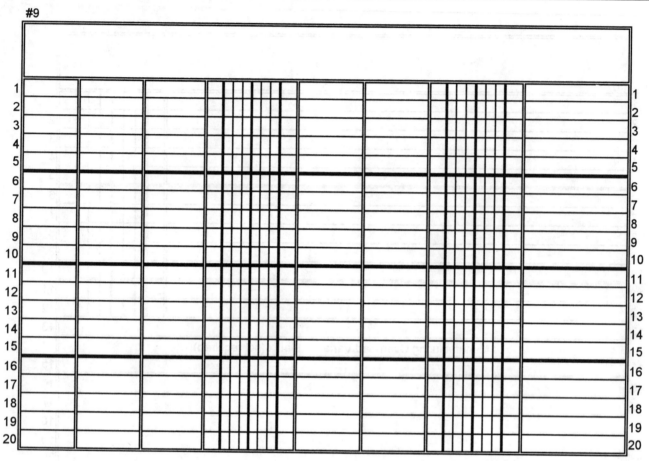

#10

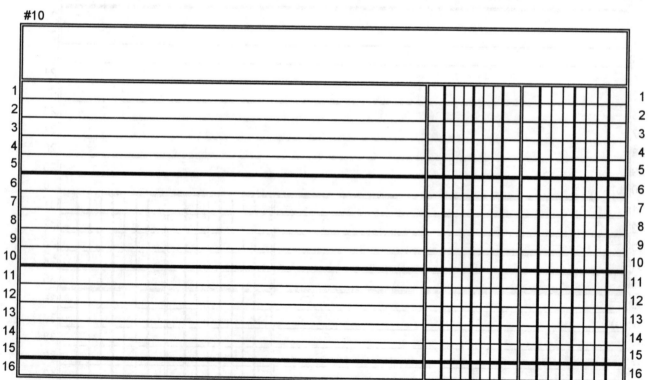

1	(1)Total materials variance:					1
2						2
3						3
4						4
5	Materials price variance:					5
6						6
7						7
8						8
9	Materials quantity variance:					9
10						10
11						11
12						12
13	(2) Total labor variance:					13
14						14
15						15
16						16
17	Labor price variance:					17
18						18
19						19
20						20
21	Labor quantity variance:					21
22						22
23						23
24						24
25	(3) Total overhead variance:					25
26						26
27						27
28						28
29	Overhead controllable variance:					29
30						30
31						31
32						32
33	Overhead volume variance:					33
34						34
35						35
36						36
37						37
38						38
39						39
40						40

(b)

Account Titles and Explanation	Debit	Credit
1		
2		
3		
4		
5		
6		
7		
8		
9		
10		
11		
12		
13		
14		
15		
16		
17		
18		
19		
20		

(c)

1	
2	
3	
4	
5	
6	
7	
8	
9	
10	
11	
12	
13	
14	
15	

(c)

Account Titles and Explanation	Debit	Credit
1		
2		
3		
4		
5		
6		
7		
8		
9		
10		
11		
12		
13		
14		
15		

(d)

WALTON CORPORATION

Income Statement

For The Month Ended January 31, 2003

1		
2		
3		
4		
5		
6		
7		
8		
9		
10		
11		
12		
13		
14		
15		
16		
17		
18		
19		
20		

(a)

1	Total materials variance:	
2		
3		
4		
5	Materials price variance:	
6		
7		
8		
9	Materials quantity variance:	
10		
11		
12		
13	Total labor variance:	
14		
15		
16		
17	Labor price variance:	
18		
19		
20		
21	Labor quantity variance:	
22		
23		
24		
25	Total overhead variance:	
26		
27		
28		
29	Overhead controllable variance:	
30		
31		
32		
33	Overhead volume variance:	
34		
35		
36		
37		
38		
39		
40		

(b)

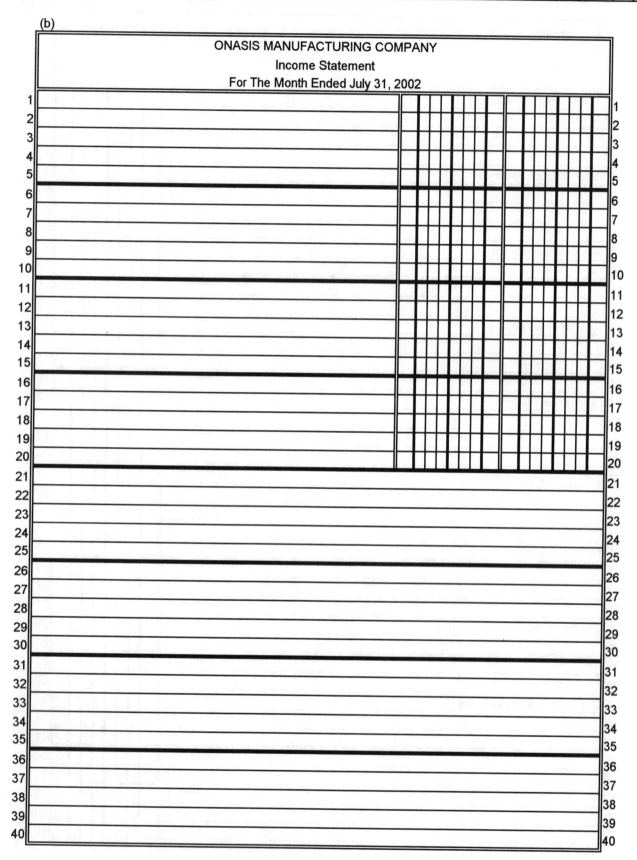

ONASIS MANUFACTURING COMPANY

Income Statement

For The Month Ended July 31, 2002

1	Total materials variance:	1
2		2
3		3
4		4
5	Materials price variance:	5
6		6
7		7
8		8
9	Materials quantity variance:	9
10		10
11		11
12		12
13	Total labor variance:	13
14		14
15		15
16		16
17	Labor price variance:	17
18		18
19		19
20		20
21	Labor quantity variance:	21
22		22
23		23
24		24
25	Total overhead variance:	25
26		26
27		27
28		28
29	Overhead controllable variance:	29
30		30
31		31
32		32
33	Overhead volume variance:	33
34		34
35		35
36		36
37		37
38		38
39		39
40		40

(1)Total materials variance:		
Materials price variance:		
Materials quantity variance:		
(2) Total labor variance:		
Labor price variance:		
Labor quantity variance:		
(3) Total overhead variance:		
Overhead controllable variance:		
Overhead volume variance:		

(b)

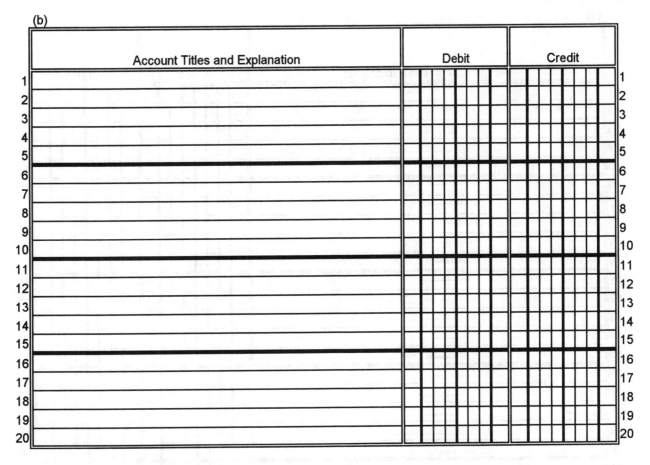

	Account Titles and Explanation	Debit	Credit	
1				1
2				2
3				3
4				4
5				5
6				6
7				7
8				8
9				9
10				10
11				11
12				12
13				13
14				14
15				15
16				16
17				17
18				18
19				19
20				20

(c)

1		1
2		2
3		3
4		4
5		5
6		6
7		7
8		8
9		9
10		10
11		11
12		12
13		13
14		14
15		15

(a)

Account Titles and Explanation	Debit	Credit
1		
2		
3		
4		
5		
6		
7		
8		
9		
10		
11		
12		
13		
14		
15		
16		
17		
18		
19		
20		
21		
22		
23		
24		
25		
26		
27		
28		
29		
30		
31		
32		
33		
34		
35		
36		
37		
38		
39		
40		

(b)

Raw Materials Inventory	Work in Process Inventory
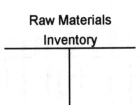	

Materials Price Variance	Materials Quantity Variance
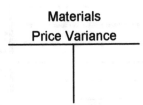	

Factory Labor	Manufacturing Overhead
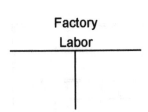	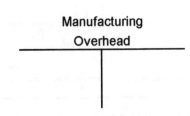

Labor Price Variance	Labor Quantity Variance
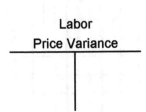	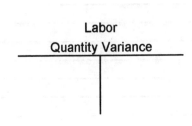

Finished Goods Inventory	Cost of Goods Sold

(c)

Account Titles and Explanation	Debit	Credit
1		
2		
3		
4		
5		
6		
7		
8		
9		
10		
11		
12		
13		
14		
15		

(d)

POMONA MANUFACTURING COMPANY
Income Statement
For The Month Ended January 31, 2002

1		
2		
3		
4		
5		
6		
7		
8		
9		
10		
11		
12		
13		
14		
15		
16		
17		
18		
19		
20		

1	1
2	2
3	3
4	4
5	5
6	6
7	7
8	8
9	9
10	10
11	11
12	12
13	13
14	14
15	15
16	16
17	17
18	18
19	19
20	20
21	21
22	22
23	23
24	24
25	25
26	26
27	27
28	28
29	29
30	30
31	31
32	32
33	33
34	34
35	35
36	36
37	37
38	38
39	39
40	40

1		1
2		2
3		3
4		4
5		5
6		6
7		7
8		8
9		9
10		10
11		11
12		12
13		13
14		14
15		15
16		16
17		17
18		18
19		19
20		20
21		21
22		22
23		23
24		24
25		25
26		26
27		27
28		28
29		29
30		30
31		31
32		32
33		33
34		34
35		35
36		36
37		37
38		38
39		39
40		40

1	1
2	2
3	3
4	4
5	5
6	6
7	7
8	8
9	9
10	10
11	11
12	12
13	13
14	14
15	15
16	16
17	17
18	18
19	19
20	20
21	21
22	22
23	23
24	24
25	25
26	26
27	27
28	28
29	29
30	30
31	31
32	32
33	33
34	34
35	35
36	36
37	37
38	38
39	39
40	40

Name

Section

Date

	1
1	1
2	2
3	3
4	4
5	5
6	6
7	7
8	8
9	9
10	10
11	11
12	12
13	13
14	14
15	15
16	16
17	17
18	18
19	19
20	20
21	21
22	22
23	23
24	24
25	25
26	26
27	27
28	28
29	29
30	30
31	31
32	32
33	33
34	34
35	35
36	36
37	37
38	38
39	39
40	40

1	1
2	2
3	3
4	4
5	5
6	6
7	7
8	8
9	9
10	10
11	11
12	12
13	13
14	14
15	15
16	16
17	17
18	18
19	19
20	20
21	21
22	22
23	23
24	24
25	25
26	26
27	27
28	28
29	29
30	30
31	31
32	32
33	33
34	34
35	35
36	36
37	37
38	38
39	39
40	40

1	1
2	2
3	3
4	4
5	5
6	6
7	7
8	8
9	9
10	10
11	11
12	12
13	13
14	14
15	15
16	16
17	17
18	18
19	19
20	20
21	21
22	22
23	23
24	24
25	25
26	26
27	27
28	28
29	29
30	30
31	31
32	32
33	33
34	34
35	35
36	36
37	37
38	38
39	39
40	40

Name

Section

Date

1											1
2											2
3											3
4											4
5											5
6											6
7											7
8											8
9											9
10											10
11											11
12											12
13											13
14											14
15											15
16											16
17											17
18											18
19											19
20											20
21											21
22											22
23											23
24											24
25											25
26											26
27											27
28											28
29											29
30											30
31											31
32											32
33											33
34											34
35											35
36											36
37											37
38											38
39											39
40											40

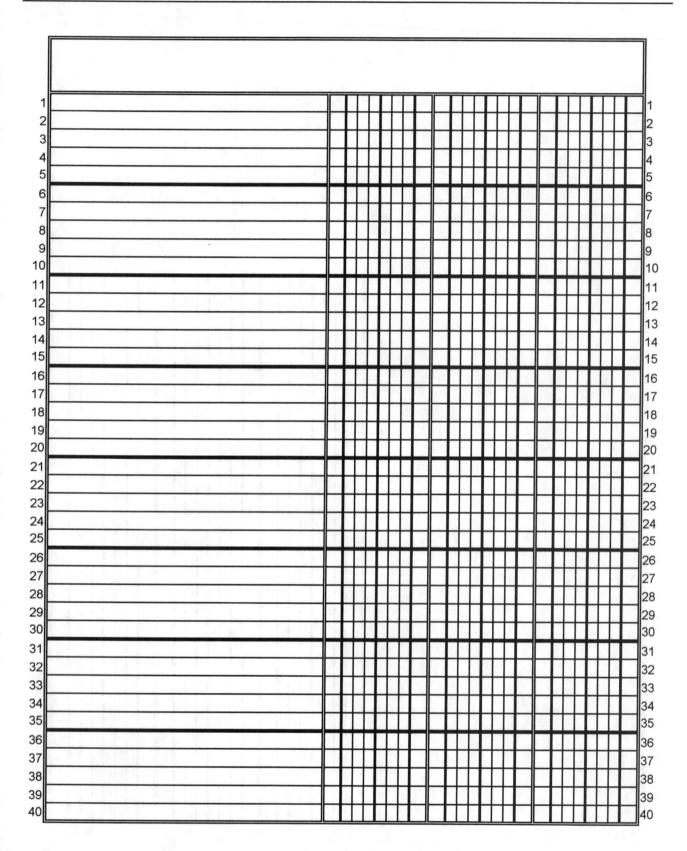

Name

Section

Date

1				1
2				2
3				3
4				4
5				5
6				6
7				7
8				8
9				9
10				10
11				11
12				12
13				13
14				14
15				15
16				16
17				17
18				18
19				19
20				20
21				21
22				22
23				23
24				24
25				25
26				26
27				27
28				28
29				29
30				30
31				31
32				32
33				33
34				34
35				35
36				36
37				37
38				38
39				39
40				40

Name

Section

Date

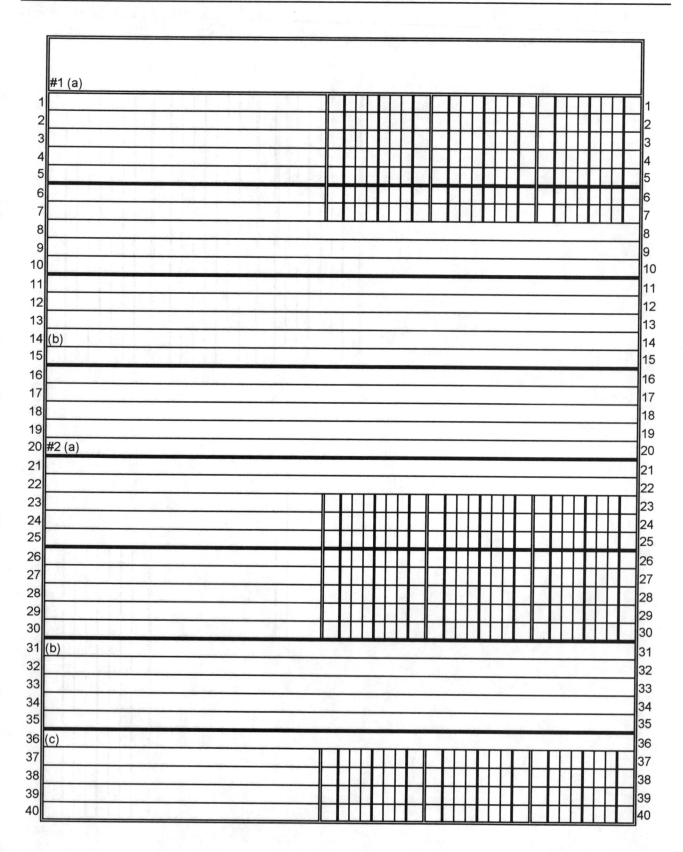

#1 (a)

(b)

#2 (a)

(b)

(c)

#3

#4

(c)

Name

Section

Date

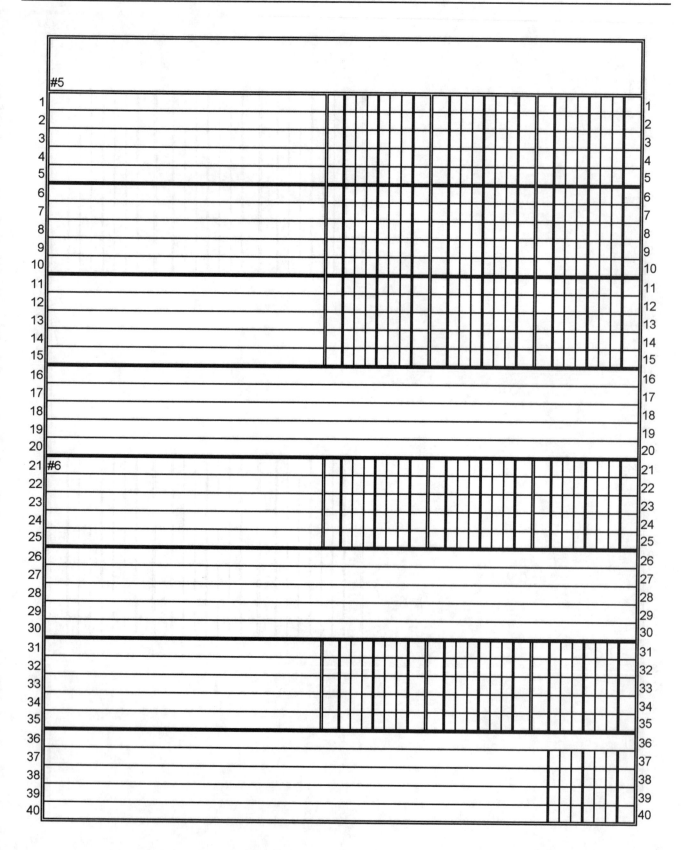

#5

#6

Name

Section

Date

#7

#8

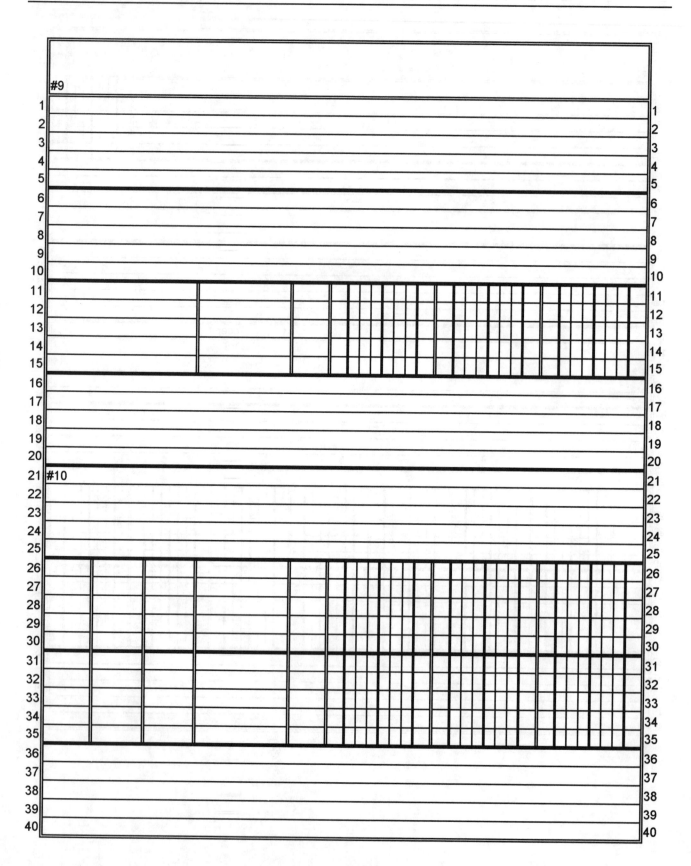

#9

#10

(a)

	Boston	Tacoma
1		
2		
3		
4		
5		
6		
7		

(b)

(1) Boston Division	Continue	Eliminate	Net Income Increase (Decrease)
1			
2			
3			
4			
5			
6			
7			
8 (2) Tacoma Division			
9			
10			
11			
12			
13			
14			
15			
16			
17			
18			
19			
20			
21			
22			
23			
24			
25			
26			
27			
28			

(c)

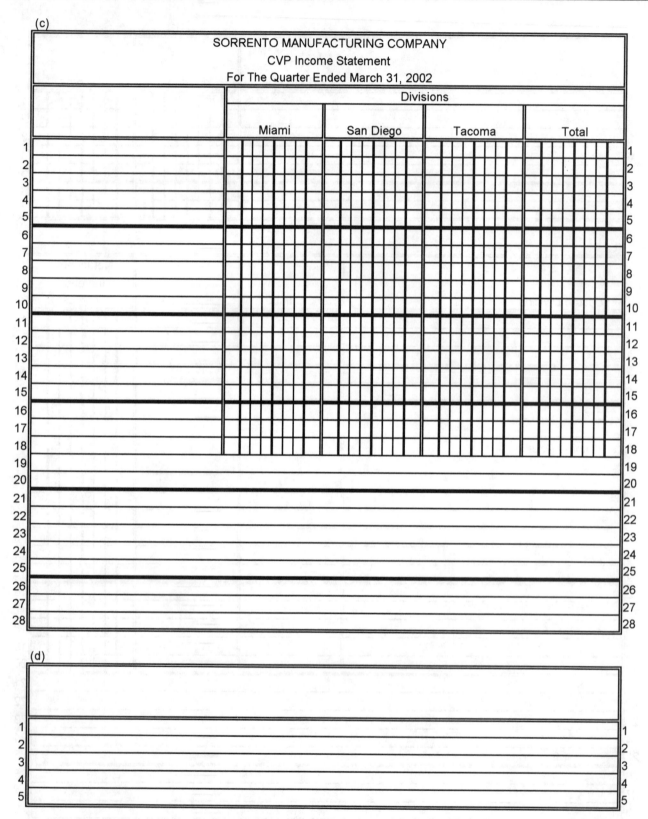

		Divisions			
		Miami	San Diego	Tacoma	Total
1					
2					
3					
4					
5					
6					
7					
8					
9					
10					
11					
12					
13					
14					
15					
16					
17					
18					
19					
20					
21					
22					
23					
24					
25					
26					
27					
28					

SORRENTO MANUFACTURING COMPANY
CVP Income Statement
For The Quarter Ended March 31, 2002

(d)

1	
2	
3	
4	
5	

(a)

	(1) Annual Net Income	(2) Annual Cash Inflow
1		
2		
3		
4		
5		
6		
7		
8		
9		
10		

(b), (c), and (d)

1	(b) (1) Annual Rate of Return:
2	
3	
4	
5	
6	(2) Cash Payback Period:
7	
8	
9	
10	
11	(c) Present Value:
12	
13	
14	
15	
16	
17	(d)
18	
19	
20	
21	
22	
23	
24	
25	

(a)

	Reject Order	Accept Order	Net Income Increase (Decrease)
1			
2			
3			
4			
5			
6			
7			
8			
9			
10			

11
12
13
14
15
16
17
18
19
20
21
22
23
24
25

(b)

26
27
28
29
30

(c)

31
32
33
34
35

(d)

36
37
38
39
40

(a)

	Make WISCO	Buy WISCO	Net Income Increase (Decrease)
1			
2			
3			
4			
5			
6			
7			
8			
9			
10			
11			
12			

(b)

(c)

	Make WISCO	Buy WISCO	Net Income Increase (Decrease)
26			
27			
28			
29			
30			

(d)

(a)

	Division III	Division IV
1		
2		
3		
4		
5		
6		
7		

(b)

(1) Division III	Continue	Eliminate	Net Income Increase (Decrease)
1			
2			
3			
4			
5			
6			
7			
8			
9			
10 (2) Division IV			
11			
12			
13			
14			
15			
16			
17			
18			
19			
20			
21			
22			
23			
24			
25			
26			
27			
28			

(c)

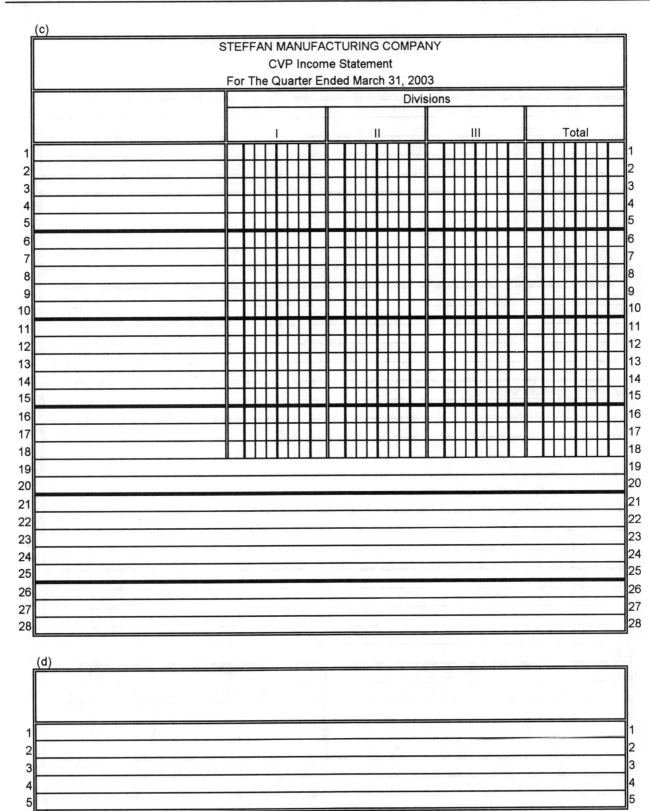

STEFFAN MANUFACTURING COMPANY
CVP Income Statement
For The Quarter Ended March 31, 2003

	Divisions			
	I	II	III	Total

(d)

(a), (b), and (d)

1	(a) Average Annual Rate of Return:
2	
3	
4	
5	
6	
7	
8	
9	
10	
11	
12	
13	
14	
15	
16	(b) Cash Payback Period:
17	
18	
19	
20	
21	
22	
23	
24	
25	
26	
27	
28	
29	
30	(d)

Project	Average Annual Rate of Return	Cash Payback Period	Net Present Value

(c)

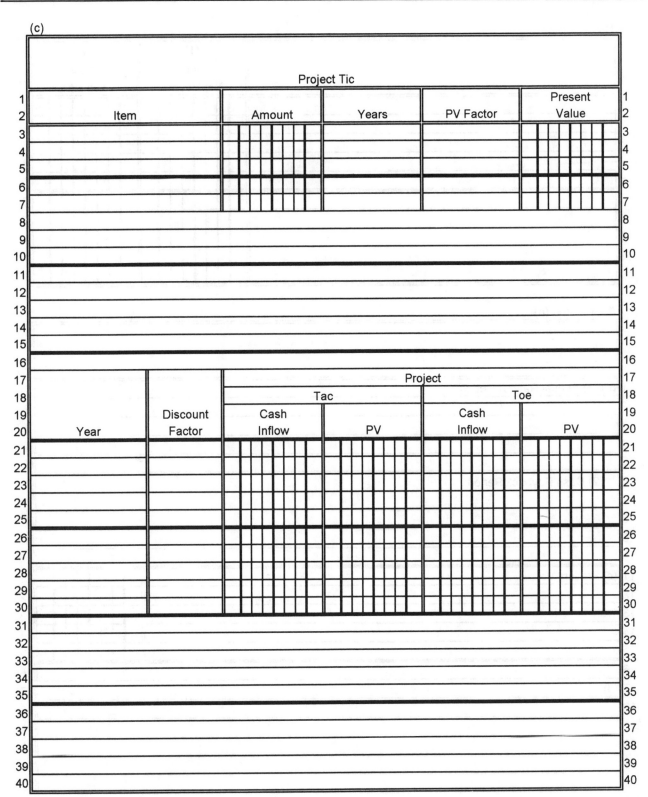

	Project Tic				
Item	Amount	Years	PV Factor	Present Value	

		Project				
		Tac		Toe		
Year	Discount Factor	Cash Inflow	PV	Cash Inflow	PV	

(a)

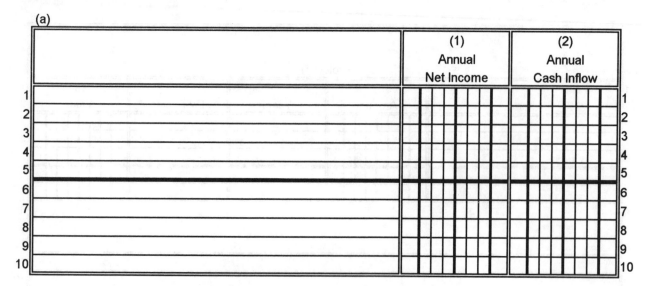

	(1) Annual Net Income	(2) Annual Cash Inflow
1		
2		
3		
4		
5		
6		
7		
8		
9		
10		

(b), (c), and (d)

1	(b) (1) Annual Rate of Return:	
2		
3		
4		
5		
6	(2) Cash Payback Period:	
7		
8		
9		
10		
11	(c) Present Value:	
12		
13		
14		
15		
16		
17	(d)	
18		
19		
20		
21		
22		
23		
24		
25		

Name _____

Section _____

Date _____ Bicycle Helmet Company

(a), (b), and (c)

	Item	Product Costs			Period Costs
		Direct Materials	Direct Labor	Mfg Overhead	
1					
2					
3					
4					
5					
6					
7					
8					
9					
10					
11					
12					
13					
14					
15					
16					
17					
18					
19					
20					
21	(e)				
22					
23					
24					
25					
26	(f)				
27					
28					
29					
30					
31					
32					
33					
34					
35					
36					
37					
38					
39					
40					

(d) and (g)

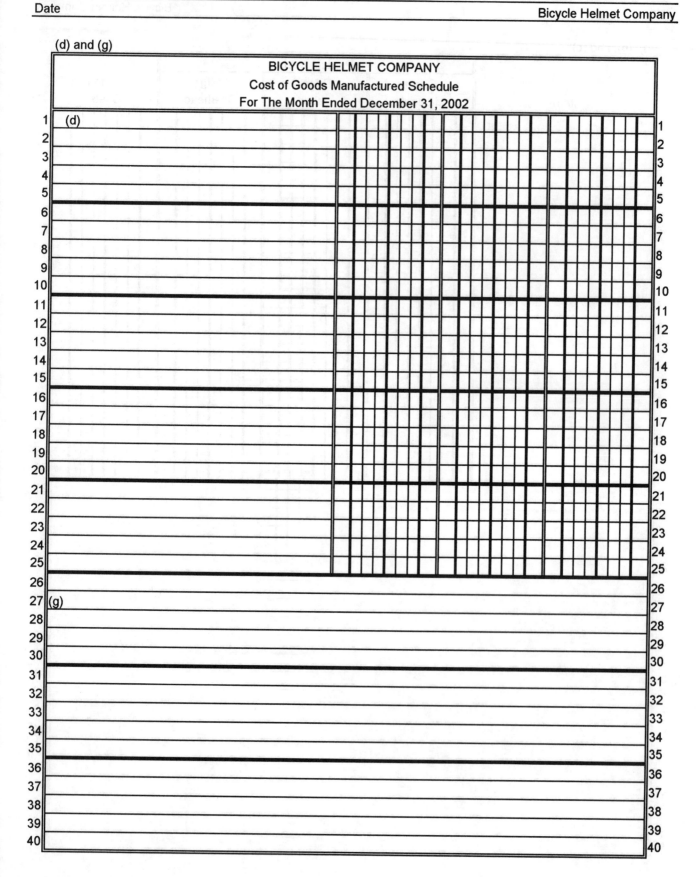

BICYCLE HELMET COMPANY

Cost of Goods Manufactured Schedule

For The Month Ended December 31, 2002

(d)

(g)

(h), (l), and (j)

(h) Item	Variable Costs	Fixed Costs	Total Costs
1			
2			
3			
4			
5			
6			
7			
8			
9			
10			
11			
12			
13			
14			
15			
16			
17			
18			
19			
20			
21			
22			
23			
24			
25			
26 (l)			
27			
28			
29 (j)			
30			
31			
32			
33			
34			
35			
36			
37			
38			
39			
40			

(k)

	1
1	
2	
3	
4	
5	
6	
7	
8	
9	
10	
11	
12	
13	
14	
15	

(l)

BICYCLE HELMET COMPANY
Sales Budget
For The Month Ended December 31, 2002

	1
1	
2	
3	
4	
5	

BICYCLE HELMET COMPANY
Production Budget
For The Month Ended December 31, 2002

	1
1	
2	
3	
4	
5	
6	
7	
8	
9	
10	

(l) Continued

| BICYCLE HELMET COMPANY |
| Direct Materials Budget |
| For The Month Ended December 31, 2002 |

1	
2	
3	
4	
5	
6	
7	
8	
9	
10	

| BICYCLE HELMET COMPANY |
| Direct Labor Budget |
| For The Month Ended December 31, 2002 |

1	
2	
3	
4	
5	
6	

| BICYCLE HELMET COMPANY |
| Selling and Administrative Expense Budget |
| For The Month Ended December 31, 2002 |

1	
2	
3	
4	
5	

(l) Continued

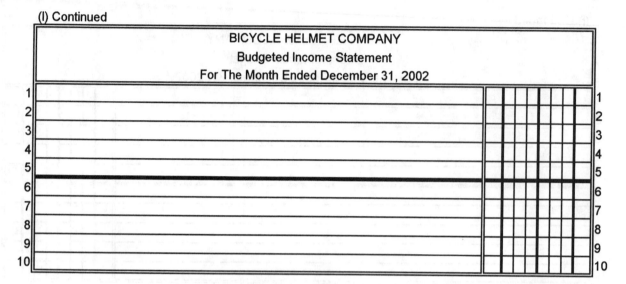

BICYCLE HELMET COMPANY
Budgeted Income Statement
For The Month Ended December 31, 2002

(m)

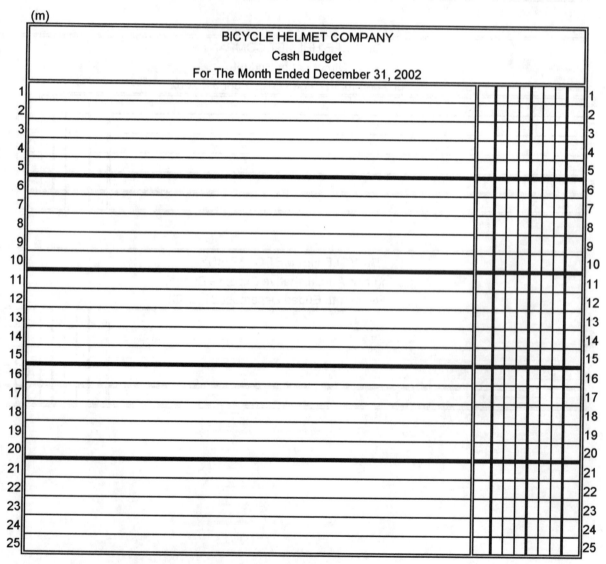

BICYCLE HELMET COMPANY
Cash Budget
For The Month Ended December 31, 2002

(n)

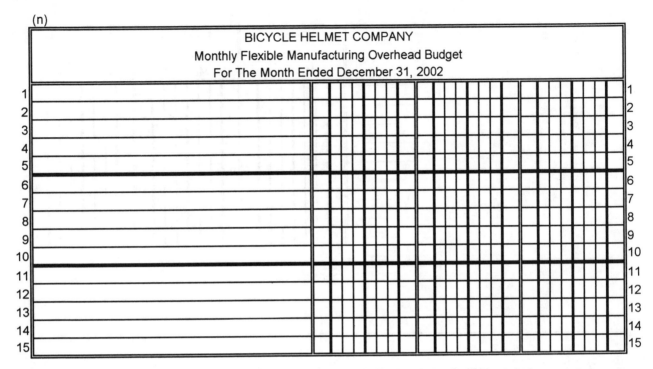

| BICYCLE HELMET COMPANY |
| Monthly Flexible Manufacturing Overhead Budget |
| For The Month Ended December 31, 2002 |

(o), (p), and (q)

(o)

(p)

(q)

(a)

	Retain Old Machine	Purchase New Machine	Net Income Increase (Decrease)
1			
2			
3			
4			
5			
6			
7			
8			
9			
10			
11			
12			
13			
14			

(b), (c), and (e)

(b) Annual Rate of Return:

1
2
3

(c) Cash Payback Pedriod:

4
5
6

(e)

7
8
9
10
11
12

(d)

	Amount	PV Factor	Present Value
1			
2			
3			
4			

(a)

	Make	Buy Silver Star	Buy Alpha
1			
2			
3			
4			
5			
6			
7			
8			
9			
10			
11			
12			
13			
14			
15			
16			
17			
18			
19			
20			
21			
22			
23			
24			
25			

(b)

26	
27	
28	
29	
30	
31	
32	
33	
34	
35	
36	
37	
38	
39	
40	

(c)

Name

Section

Date

1	1
2	2
3	3
4	4
5	5
6	6
7	7
8	8
9	9
10	10
11	11
12	12
13	13
14	14
15	15

Name

Section

Date

	1		1
	2		2
	3		3
	4		4
	5		5
	6		6
	7		7
	8		8
	9		9
	10		10
	11		11
	12		12
	13		13
	14		14
	15		15
	16		16
	17		17
	18		18
	19		19
	20		20
	21		21
	22		22
	23		23
	24		24
	25		25
	26		26
	27		27
	28		28
	29		29
	30		30
	31		31
	32		32
	33		33
	34		34
	35		35
	36		36
	37		37
	38		38
	39		39
	40		40

	1		1
	2		2
	3		3
	4		4
	5		5
	6		6
	7		7
	8		8
	9		9
	10		10
	11		11
	12		12
	13		13
	14		14
	15		15
	16		16
	17		17
	18		18
	19		19
	20		20
	21		21
	22		22
	23		23
	24		24
	25		25
	26		26
	27		27
	28		28
	29		29
	30		30
	31		31
	32		32
	33		33
	34		34
	35		35
	36		36
	37		37
	38		38
	39		39
	40		40

1	1
2	2
3	3
4	4
5	5
6	6
7	7
8	8
9	9
10	10
11	11
12	12
13	13
14	14
15	15
16	16
17	17
18	18
19	19
20	20
21	21
22	22
23	23
24	24
25	25
26	26
27	27
28	28
29	29
30	30
31	31
32	32
33	33
34	34
35	35
36	36
37	37
38	38
39	39
40	40

	1
1	
2	2
3	3
4	4
5	5
6	6
7	7
8	8
9	9
10	10
11	11
12	12
13	13
14	14
15	15
16	16
17	17
18	18
19	19
20	20
21	21
22	22
23	23
24	24
25	25
26	26
27	27
28	28
29	29
30	30
31	31
32	32
33	33
34	34
35	35
36	36
37	37
38	38
39	39
40	40

Name

Date

		1
1		1
2		2
3		3
4		4
5		5
6		6
7		7
8		8
9		9
10		10
11		11
12		12
13		13
14		14
15		15
16		16
17		17
18		18
19		19
20		20
21		21
22		22
23		23
24		24
25		25
26		26
27		27
28		28
29		29
30		30
31		31
32		32
33		33
34		34
35		35
36		36
37		37
38		38
39		39
40		40

1		1
2		2
3		3
4		4
5		5
6		6
7		7
8		8
9		9
10		10
11		11
12		12
13		13
14		14
15		15
16		16
17		17
18		18
19		19
20		20
21		21
22		22
23		23
24		24
25		25
26		26
27		27
28		28
29		29
30		30
31		31
32		32
33		33
34		34
35		35
36		36
37		37
38		38
39		39
40		40

1	1
2	2
3	3
4	4
5	5
6	6
7	7
8	8
9	9
10	10
11	11
12	12
13	13
14	14
15	15
16	16
17	17
18	18
19	19
20	20
21	21
22	22
23	23
24	24
25	25
26	26
27	27
28	28
29	29
30	30
31	31
32	32
33	33
34	34
35	35
36	36
37	37
38	38
39	39
40	40